OUT OF THE
LABYRINTH

OUT OF THE
LABYRINTH

─FOR THOSE WHO WANT TO BELIEVE BUT CAN'T─

J. DONALD WALTERS

Cover and book design by
C. A. Starner Schuppe and Helen Strang

Cover photo of NGC 4414 courtesy of NASA

ISBN: 1-56589-148-1
Printed in Canada

Crystal

Clarity

Crystal Clarity Publishers
14618 Tyler-Foote Road
Nevada City, CA 95959-8599

Phone: 800-424-1055 or 530-478-7600
Fax: 530-478-7610
E-mail: clarity@crystalclarity.com
Website: www.crystalclarity.com

Library of Congress Cataloging-in-Publication Data

Walters, J. Donald.
  Out of the labyrinth / J. Donald Walters.-- Rev., 3rd ed.
    p. cm.
  Rev. ed. of: Crises in modern thought. 1988.
  Includes bibliographical references and index.
  ISBN 1-56589-148-1 (pbk.)
    1. Spiritual life. 2. Meaning (Philosophy) 3. Philosophy and
science.   I. Walters, J. Donald. Crises in modern thought. II. Title.
  BP605.S4 W355 2001
  190--dc21

                                    2001042499

*This book is dedicated
not to a person,
but to a purpose:
the spread of light, where
there has been confusion.*

CONTENTS

FOREWORD

I HAVE FOUND THIS BOOK ENTHRALLING TO READ. Never before have I encountered such a clear explanation of the limitations of traditional philosophy in its relation to the advancement of science. *Out of the Labyrinth* presents an entirely new and liberating framework for relating to reality. It connects philosophy directly to modern science and to natural law. With great clarity J. Donald Walters offers an alternative to old forms of rationalism, which have found themselves in forced retirement owing to the advances of modern science.

Several years ago I taught a university course that included a review of Western philosophy. When the time came for a discussion of values, I was amazed to find that most of my brightest students airily dismissed the subject as "relative." Further probing on my part revealed that they equated values with dogmatism, and dogmatism with intolerance. Values, therefore, to their way of thinking, represented the antithesis of what they considered the primary contribution of modern education: open-mindedness.

These students pointed to past wars, racism, religious dogmatism, sexism, and—most significantly—to the more recent developments of science which, they believed, negate the very existence of absolute values.

My students weren't smug or jaded. In fact, they earnestly sought a way out of the dilemma that this book identifies: the "loss of focus on familiar ethical and spiritual guidelines: truth, honor, and justice." Had *Out of the Labyrinth* been available then, I would have made it required reading. Not only does it do a superior job of clarifying the often-confusing history of Western philosophy, but it offers a radical and obvious solution to the all-too-prevalent attraction of nihilism.

No other work with which I am familiar actually connects the scientific approach to serious philosophical inquiry, as this work does outstandingly. Walters proves that values do in fact exist, but that they exist in the natural order, and in laws that govern not only nature, but human conduct as well.

Out of the Labyrinth builds bridges. It is not a work of firework polemics, but succeeds instead in calmly, with patent common sense, reconciling what others before now have considered irreconcilable differences. Walters takes a profound subject and turns it from the dry dissertation that it might so easily have become into a process of joyous sharing. His remarkable ability to see connections, where others have seen only contradictions, makes it possible for him, and for the reader in his turn, to view things from an extraordinarily broad perspective.

This book never challenges the findings of science. Rather, it places those findings in a completely new light. Walters validates the fluidity of relativity, as an example, by merging it with human experience, and even with the biological sciences. Relativity, he maintains, has meaning. For one reason, it implies relationships, not chaos. For another, and he makes this point carefully, while values are not absolute they *are* universal. He shows that relative development is not vague and uncertain, but directional and progressive. He ends up making the case that relativity actually deepens "our overall sense of living in a richly meaningful universe."

In his study of evolution, Walters establishes a completely new and exciting view of natural selection. He provides the reader with an expansive and relativistic vision that surmounts traditional identification with matter and makes a tight case for his claim that the ultimate reality of the universe is pure consciousness.

Walters has created a wonderful as well as an aesthetically pleasing work with this book. Einstein, it is reported, wouldn't work on equations that weren't beautiful. Beauty, for Einstein, meant a quality of energy, a refinement of focus. The purity of thought in *Out of the Labyrinth* approaches the perfection that Einstein sought and appreciated. Like the composer of a symphony, J. Donald Walters develops various aspects of human experience in criss-crossing themes that produce harmony, beauty, and glory that will be a delight for all readers who are willing to practice the open-mindedness that was so praised by those ex-students of mine.

Jay J. Casbon, Ph.D.
Dean of the Graduate School, Lewis & Clark College

INTRODUCTION

DURING THE PROCESS of writing this book, I paid a visit to the eminent Jewish scholar, Dr. Leon Kolb, who had been recommended to me as an expert on the history of the Jewish people. I was hoping that he would be able to endorse a point I wanted to make in my section on evolution.

As it happened, although he helped me, it was more in the negative sense: He recounted certain facts of history which forced me to abandon my point.

As our conversation progressed, however, a response that was initially negative on his part ended up very positively indeed for the larger issues of the book.

I had mentioned to Dr. Kolb why I was writing this book, which I said combatted with new ideas the modern question of meaninglessness. By way of illustrating why life is so widely considered meaningless, I mentioned the claim of modern biologists that evolution is purely accidental.

"But it *is* accidental!" he cried indignantly, interrupting my explanation. "Completely accidental!" He went on to inform me that he was not only a Jewish scholar, but an anthropologist, and had taught physiology at Stanford University for thirty years until his recent retirement. He was solidly in the camp of the evolutionists.

"Perhaps," I suggested, "you'd like to read my chapters titled, 'Meaning in Evolution'?"

"It's accidental, I tell you. Biologists are all quite agreed on the subject."

"But I haven't disagreed with them!" I replied.

He looked non-plussed. "Then how can you talk of *meaning* in evolution?"

"My approach," I said, "is probably so different from any you've come across that I think you might really enjoy reading it. And I'd certainly appreciate any corrections you might care to make in it, if you can find any fault with what I've written."

"Very well," he agreed, somewhat reluctantly, "I'll read what you've written. But it's useless, I tell you. Evolution is completely accidental!"

I visited him again a week later to see how much of my work, if any, he'd read. His eyes as he greeted me at the door were fairly shining with excitement.

"But this is wonderful!" he exclaimed. "It's completely in harmony with the findings of modern science, yet it provides them with deep *meaning*. It is wonderful—*wonderful!* I tell you, this message must be spread everywhere!"

I hope other readers will confirm his reaction. For the subject matter treated here is vitally important to the present state of our civilization. Too many people have had their confidence in life's meaning and purpose shaken by the insistence of so many of today's thinkers that life is meaningless.

My purpose in writing this book has not been to discuss at length the intricacies of Western philosophy, nor indeed to familiarize myself with all of them. Sartre enthusiasts, for example, might complain, "Oh, but *else-where* in his writings Sartre says such-and-so." More power to him, I reply, but *this* is most certainly what he said in those writings with which I've dealt here. It wouldn't alter my purpose if, since then, he had completely changed his mind (although in fact he did not). It is the ideas he expressed that I have challenged, not the man himself. It is those ideas which, in this Twentieth Century, have become so widespread. I have made Sartre my target only because he expressed them so lucidly.

Please, then, approach this book as a fresh statement—or, if you like, as an approach from a new angle. Don't try to determine out of which school of Western thought it might have sprung, for it owes its solutions to none of them. And remember that it takes time to make a difficult point. Please, therefore, hear me out before rebutting me, should rebuttal come instinctively to you.

For just as Dr. Kolb thought I meant to say one thing only to find that my meaning was very different, so anyone who is familiar with the currents of modern thought will be tempted to jump in at the beginning with assumptions that have no bearing on my actual argument.

With that let me conclude: "Dear Reader, allow me to present my good friend, This Book. Now, with your permission I'll just leave the two of you alone together to chat for awhile. I hope you'll find that you have lots in common."

PREFACE
TO THE 1988 (REVISED) EDITION

I BEGAN PLANNING this book in 1962. The research for it, and then the writing and the revision, covered the next ten years. Another sixteen years have passed since the book was first published. During all this time I have pondered the subjects covered, and refined my ideas regarding them. Hence, twenty-six years after those first beginnings, but with no lessening of enthusiasm for the subject, this revised edition.

Out of the Labyrinth is essentially a work of philosophy, not of science. It deals with facts of human nature that are essentially changeless, and relates them to findings of science and to statements by other thinkers that, although no longer of recent date, are by no means out of date. Indeed, all the themes developed in these pages are as fresh today as they were twenty-six years ago. While the thoughts are presented more clearly and simply in this edition, therefore, I have not considered it necessary to enlist further scientific evidence in their support. If a painting is well planned and executed, with a proper balance of color and design, it would merely detract from its beauty to add new pigments simply because they had been more recently invented.

PREFACE
TO THE THIRD (2001) EDITION

TWELVE MORE YEARS have passed since the Second Edition. This book might almost pass as a definition of my life! It has been important to me, for it was not only my first serious attempt to present these truths to the modern mind, but also, to a large extent, forms the basis of everything I have written since then.

I have felt for some time that a new title was needed. I have changed the title, accordingly, from *Crises in Modern Thought* to *Out of the Labyrinth* as a more dynamic expression of the insights it contains. I have also re-edited the last chapter to make its last pages easier to read.

In all these years, from 1962–2001, this has remained, for me, an important contribution to the quest for clarity in modern thinking. It hasn't sold particularly well, a fact I regret. My own faith in it, however, has remained undiminished.

OUT OF THE
LABYRINTH

CHAPTER ONE

The Crises

Twentieth-Century science has showered mankind with blessings. It has brought him material ease, and expanded his mental horizons. But it has also brought him great mental uneasiness, and a gradual loss of focus on familiar ethical and spiritual guidelines—"truth, honor, and justice"—which have been the bulwark of every great civilization of the past. Absolutes now seem to be an unattainable dream. Our present is a new and unfamiliar world of relativities. It is important that we find some meaningful substitute for our lost sense of meaning.

CHAPTER ONE

The Crises

IT IS COMMONLY ACCEPTED that we are living in an age of crisis. The signs can be seen everywhere: in the grim global opposition of incompatible social ideologies; in the spiritual confusion that has been stirred up by modern science; in the challenge to old moral concepts of a cynical, and growing, amorality; in a way of life whose frenzied pace is assaulting our very sanity. We talk of peace, yet know in our hearts that peace is not a natural offspring of nervousness, fear, and doubt. We talk of prosperity, yet spend ourselves into worrisome debt. We cry "Liberty!", yet equate this ideal with the freedom of other men to be exactly like—but only like—ourselves. We praise equality, yet the very word is often made a penalty for excellence, and "togetherness" becomes a slogan with which initiative is subdued.

Science, bestower of so many blessings, has brought us also what may be the greatest test mankind has ever faced. The problem is not whether scientific progress will be the cause of man's destruction. At stake, rather, is our ability to match outward achievement with inner enlightenment.

Humanity in its present danger may be compared to an imperfectly balanced flywheel, which serves well enough so long as its turning is slow, but may be shaken to pieces as its speed increases. Scientific progress will very possibly spin us to destruction, if the imbalances in human nature are not corrected as conscientiously as mistakes are in mechanics, or in the physics laboratory.

The vital question is, can these imbalances be corrected?

Goals can at least be worked toward if we consider them attainable. But what if we are convinced, instead, that they do not even exist? Even those most objective of men, the dedicated scientists, labor as patiently as they do only because of their faith in the *possibility* of achievement. It would be ridiculous to struggle if one were certain that all struggle was futile.

It is here that we find the core of our contemporary difficulty. We speak of the need to grow, morally and spiritually, but while talking earnestly of "new values," we find a growing suspicion, voiced more and more frequently, that in fact there are *no* values. Our long-held view of a universe that is governed by Right is being challenged by a contradictory concept of a universe that is not governed at all—a universe that is essentially irrational and meaningless.

What final meaning, indeed, are we to ascribe to a scheme of things in which all the once-fixed "realities" are found to exist merely as relativities—in which time itself has no absolute definition? (Einstein's discovery that time is relative signifies that a young man might, conceivably, travel in a space ship to some distant star and return still in his youth, to find the contemporaries he left behind him aging or dead. A voyage that required only a year according to his reckoning might have consumed forty years here on earth.)

Euclidean geometry, the crystal logic of which was for centuries considered a "necessity of thought" and a virtual proof of the perfection of God's law, is no longer seen as a logical necessity at all. A hundred years ago, Lobachevsky and Bolyai, working separately, proved that quite different, and perfectly self-consistent, systems can be built on other sets of axioms.

One of the new geometric systems that resulted from this discovery, that of the German mathematician, Riemann, conceives the vastness of space as actually finite. Scientific men are convinced that space really is governed by Riemann's geometry, and not by Euclid's.

To the natural question, "If space is finite, what's outside of it?" the scientist's answer is, "Nothing. You are applying human preconceptions to a situation where they do not obtain."* What earthly sense can we make of such an inconceivable scheme of things?

The longstanding argument as to whether light is a particle or a wave has at last been resolved in a hopeless (but proved) contradiction: It is both.

Where, indeed, is the plain, "down-to-earth" logic of a universe in which the earth doesn't seem to exist at all? Or, if it exists, what is it? Not only a near vacuum—its atomic particles as distant from one another,

---

* See J.W.N. Sullivan, *The Limitations of Science* (New York, Mentor Books, 1959), pp. 19, 20.

relatively speaking, as the stars in the heavens—but the particles themselves are evanescent: energy, not solid substance. The eminent scientist, Sir Arthur Stanley Eddington, called them mind-stuff, not even energy.*

Science today tells us that the categories of reason, far from being absolutes, are a sort of elaborate mythology in which words and concepts have meaning primarily as we *give* them meaning. They are true within the framework we ourselves have arranged, but are not true in any fixed or eternal sense. Euclidean geometry is true in its own way, and can be applied to the construction of a building. Yet, as far as science knows, there is no such thing as a straight line, the existence of which is the very basis of Euclid's geometry.

The astounding discoveries of modern times have thrown all our accustomed thinking out of gear. Is there, one asks oneself, any absolute meaning in anything? Into what niche is one now to fit men's previous conceptions of right and wrong? Can we logically conceive of moral absolutes, when creation itself seems to be ruled "absolutely" only by relativities?

If we feel the need for some solid foundation for our morality, the physical sciences certainly seem to provide us with none.

Many thinking men today have shifted their concentration away from this seemingly chaotic cosmos to the more comforting, because limited, phenomenon of man. Their decision seems practical. After all, life for us goes on as ever. Whatever the earth's final nature, it is as solid as ever in the context of material laws and

* Sir Arthur Eddington, *The Nature of the Physical World.*

of man's own experience. Nor has Einstein's discovery of the relativity of time thrown our clocks out of kilter. If different systems of geometry can be at least *self-*consistent, we may well ask why we should not conceive of human life as some sort of self-contained "extra-geometric" system, ruled by laws that are, at least for mankind, absolute.

From a human standpoint, anyway, there might be some hope here of discovering lasting values, and thereby of defeating the depressing suggestion from science that no values exist. From our point of view, after all, there *are* such things as cooperation, honor, and honesty. There are also the opposite qualities—treachery, weakness of character, dishonesty—traits of which (we assume) all men disapprove. Perhaps it would be best for us simply to look at our own human problems in this rosy light, and with Omar Khayyam "the riddle of the universe let be."

We might indeed thus manage to leave science alone. But will science leave us alone? It hasn't done so, not by a long shot. Even on our familiar human plane, science has roused the sleeping dragons of confusion.

Since the invention of electronic computers, close parallels have been found between their function and that of the human brain. In certain respects, in fact, the only noticeable difference is that our electronic counterparts work so much faster and more efficiently than we can. (If they didn't, we wouldn't need their services.)

Electronic brains are "programmed" to think in particular channels. They function only in those channels. Human brains, likewise—so we are told—think only as they are conditioned, or "programmed," to think. The pattern is more complex, of course, but scientists claim that the parallel is exact, and that even our sudden "inspirations" are due to prior conditioning. Thinking, in other words, is considered to be simply a sort of electronic "manipulation of memory traces in the brain."

Differences in outlook, perhaps as a result of such conditioning, can reach astonishing proportions. Most of us today look upon kindness as a universal virtue. But certain primitive peoples, notably in certain parts of Africa, look upon kindness as merely a sign of cowardice.

Again, we assume that we have fairly clear notions of what it means to be brave. There are tribes in Borneo, however, that contradict all these notions. They consider it a sign of manly courage to kill the unsuspecting child of some enemy tribe with a poisoned dart from behind a tree.

There are people who believe it a virtue to steal, and still others by whom an inability to lie cleverly is viewed with scorn—not only as indicative of incompetence, which would at least be understandable, but actually (in the case of certain gypsy tribes in Tuscany) as a mark that one is without *truth!*

Obviously, from a standpoint of comparative beliefs, right and wrong are not such fixed values as we have been brought up to suppose. And this lack of fixity seems all the greater when scientists tell us that a man's beliefs can be manipulated—to what extent no one yet knows—by expert conditioning on the part of others.

Personality itself, that subtlest phenomenon of human nature, can be changed with a surgeon's knife.

Prefrontal lobotomy, the brain operation that won for its discoverer, Dr. Egaz Moniz, the Nobel prize in 1949, has been performed on countless thousands of mentally disturbed people, freeing them of anxiety, delusions, epileptic fits, and other abnormal nervous conditions. But the operation has also been found to produce definite changes in the personalities of the patients. It has made them shallower, less sensitive. Drs. Walter Freeman and James W. Watts, two leading specialists in this field, reported: "It is becoming more and more plain that patients who undergo lobotomy must sacrifice some virtues, some of the driving force, some of the uplift, altruism, creative spirit, soul or whatever else one would like to call it."*

And of course, there is that old skeptics' delight, the doctrine of evolution. Biologists today make as good a case as one can imagine for meaninglessness. They are more or less unanimous on the point that life has evolved by sheer accident, and not by any meaningful design. The findings they submit in support of their claim are innumerable.

These and other similar discoveries of our times, bolstered by those of the grander cosmic relativities, are reducing to shambles the hopes of many thinking persons of finding fixed values anywhere.

Who knows? Perhaps they are right. But if they are, what must the conclusion be?

We have seen times when, without any encouragement from objective science, large numbers of men have

* Walter Freeman and James W. Watts, *Progress in Neurology and Psychiatry* (New York, Grune and Stratton, Inc., 1948), pp. 409–20.

turned cynical about any ultimate or basic verities. The Greeks passed through such a period. So also did the Romans. So likewise, in fact, has almost every other dead civilization, and the period has always coincided with its decadence and dissolution.

Let us face it: It takes moral vigor to build a strong and peaceful society. It takes moral vigor to resist the demands of immediate ease over those of lasting fulfillment. Where is the man who, believing in nothing sincerely, will stand by anything or anyone through life's storms and trials? He will be a drifter, rather, moving with the currents of personal convenience.

No doubt the world will always have its share of cynics. Even when spiritual beliefs have been widespread, there have been men who seized power by murder, or who sold their conscience for a fat purse. But if the notion were to gain popularity that such behavior is as good, "relatively" speaking, as any other, the natural urge for pleasure and self-aggrandizement might well become as contagious as any disease. The examples of history suggest forcefully that such a notion, unchecked, might easily spread to epidemic proportions.

For men *are* their philosophies. They are swayed not so much by events as by ideas. What, then, of an age when leading thinkers, bolstered by factual evidence from the respected sciences, assure us that life is fundamentally meaningless, and that there is no real purpose in anything? Science may indeed bring us some final enlightenment, but let us hope it is not the light engendered by the Final Bomb!

For hope we must. It goes against every natural

instinct to view with aplomb the prospect of final disaster. To have faith in *nothing* would be to renounce our very humanity, and to ally ourselves with the incurious machines, clicking and buzzing our way through life absorbed only in matters of the moment.

In every respect, our crisis today may be summed up as a crisis of purpose, as a desperate search for *something* tangible in which we can truly believe. Without beliefs of some sort, and without at least *some* sense of life's meaningfulness, life itself is in danger of becoming a tortured nightmare, an anguished scream of insanity.

Yet our beliefs must be honest; they must be based on intelligent inquiry. We cannot seek refuge from unpleasant facts in mere wishful piety. Some writers have tried to do so, but theirs are not forceful voices in our age. Let us face it, belief that is no more than wishful thinking already *is* insanity.

True meanings we need now, if civilization is to be merely preserved, let alone to soar to new heights. If we can regain faith in such meaning honestly, a faith in something more tangible than the fact that we don't want to be blown to bits, or enslaved by some alien power, then and then only may we acquire the moral weapon we need to overcome the many crises now surrounding us as a people—and more than that, threatening our existence as a race.

CHAPTER TWO

Institutions
and the Individual

New insights into reality are needed if civilization is to be saved from growing cynicism and amorality, the twin destroyers of so many societies in the past. How shall we proceed in the search?

Science traditionally begins its search for universals with a study of specifics. The present search, similarly, must begin with the personal experience of man as an individual, and not with that vague entity, society. Only in man the individual can the key be found to meaning in a relative universe.

CHAPTER TWO

Institutions
and the Individual

THE PURPOSE OF THIS BOOK is not to complain at the problems science has raised concerning Ultimate Purpose and Meaning. Rather, it is to invite you, my friend and reader, on an exciting voyage of discovery.

First, I owe you a warning: This is not a voyage for the intellectually lazy. You'll be challenged to abandon many preconceptions, to expand your horizons, and perhaps to reevaluate, even drastically, certain of your life directions. The next three chapters, especially, may prove strenuous going in places. I'll be asking you to climb a steep hill with me before inviting you to ski down the other side. Throughout, however, it will be a voyage of philosophical adventure.

I won't be taking issue with science, as so many have done in their anxiety to rescue traditional values from what they view as science's attack. What I'll be doing, rather, is reinterpreting the facts from which science has worked. Where so many thinking people have drawn negative meanings from that data, I propose to show that the problem lies not in the facts themselves, but only in our understanding of them. And I'll show that they can be understood in such a way as to enrich life with meaning, and not rob it of all meaning.

If a person wants to protect his feet from getting blistered while walking a long road, he can do one of two things: get the road paved with soft rubber; or else, wear a comfortable pair of shoes. To repave the road would require a great deal of time and cost a lot of money. The simpler solution, obviously, would be to wear a comfortable pair of shoes.

The same is true if we want to remain morally unscathed while following the road to truth which modern science has pointed out to us: We can either get science to change the road, or else, we can adapt our philosophy to the demands of the journey.

To get the road changed would entail getting science to restructure its findings to meet our ethical demands. This has in fact been tried before. One thinks of the Church, for example, when it tried to get Galileo to recant his statement that the earth was not the center of the universe. But the time has passed when meddling with science was acceptable on dogmatic grounds.

Science itself, of course, is sure in time to change its views on many issues, just as it has already discarded not a few of its previous certainties. But it is from science itself that such corrections must come. For the philosopher to challenge science, he himself would have to become a scientist. His job, instead, is to help man to find the depth of understanding within himself to meet any challenge.

The shoes worn so far by Western man on his journey are no longer fit to walk in. Their soles were designed for a much shorter stroll; they were never adequate for a trek the end of which is lost to our gaze among the stars.

Science has discredited the traditional use of reason, so long considered essential to clear thinking. Aristotelian logic, which was the very foundation stone of Western thought, has been shown to be a convenience, merely, and not a necessity, of thought. In Chapter Five I'll examine the process of logic, and see whether it will not have to be adjusted in the field of ethics, as well, to the scientific mode of thinking.

Moral absolutism, again, has always been accepted in the West as the necessary basis of any true value system. Yet, in the material sphere, science has rendered absolutism obsolete. We need to consider seriously, then, whether absolutism is still tenable, or even desirable, as a philosophical concept. This I shall do in Chapter Four.

If worse comes to worst, perhaps the advance of science really does herald the death of meaning as we have always understood it. Do the findings of science force upon us a nihilistic interpretation of our relationship to one another and to the universe? In this case, it may be that each of us must carve out whatever system of values seems personally meaningful to him. At any rate, we must consider first the claims of nihilism before proceeding to a search for more positive values that will stand secure against any charge of sentimentalism or wishful thinking.

In Chapter Three I plan to examine nihilism and see whether it is as realistic a response to the discoveries of science as its proponents claim. Following the analysis of nihilism will come the examination of moral absolutism. And after moral absolutism will come our analysis of reason itself, in which we'll study the inadequacy of Aristotelian logic to cope with a universe in eternal flux.

At that point we'll have reached the top of the hill. During our ensuing downhill run we'll explore an entirely new approach to life's meaning: a fresh view of things, compatible with the expansive vision of modern science, yet at the same time one that gives life the deepest possible meaning.

To arrive at new insights, one must abandon the salon of orthodoxy where dialogues based on unquestioned assumptions take place, and step out alone into the silent night. For only here, before the immensity of time and space, is deep thought really possible. New insights cannot be born in passive reaction to the things other people have said and done. Let us therefore make up our minds from the beginning of our adventure to embrace the unknown; to think creatively for ourselves, and to have the courage to ignore the reproving cries of traditionalists who may object that to seek outside their smoke-filled salon is presumptuous.

For where is the presumption in courage? The wildflowers of fresh insight cannot grow on well-trampled paths. And truth cannot be voted into existence by popular acclaim. Truth simply *is*. It awaits discovery by those men and women only whose spirits are bold.

Several years ago, someone devised an experiment

that has since been repeated many times, always with more or less the same results. Two lines are drawn on a blackboard. The top line is notably shorter than the bottom line. Six subjects are then asked to say which of the two lines is longer.

The catch is that five of the subjects are instructed in advance to declare that the top line is the longer. The sixth subject, unaware of this conspiracy, is the last to be asked for his verdict.

The amazing outcome of this experiment is that in eighty percent of the cases the sixth subject, denying the testimony of his own eyes, agrees with the other five that the top line is the longer.

If, when faced with such blatant alternatives, eighty percent of those asked have preferred social acceptability over truthfulness, what must the percentage be when the choices are less obvious?

Egregious, a word not often heard in English, derives from two Latin words meaning, "out of the herd." In English, egregious means, "outstandingly bad." In Italian, the same Latin-derivative means "outstandingly noble and good," and is used as an honorific—a fact which I discovered in Florence several years ago, when I received a parking ticket accompanied by a letter in which I found myself addressed as "Egregio Signore." (My first thought was, "Aren't they satisfied with taking my money? Do they have to insult me as well?")

We, too, must stand "out of the herd" if we want to see things with clear vision. In doing so, we are bound to attract criticism from those who think it a sin to ignore the well-traveled highways of thought. But let us hope that it isn't only in Italy that intellectual independence is acceptable. For only if we can stand apart from the numerous ongoing dialogues on the subject can we hope to rescue meaning from the present chaos into which it has fallen.

Where values are concerned, one of two approaches is usually taken. There is, first, the approach of orthodox religionists: "The Bible has settled everything for us. It behooves not mankind to ask, 'Why?' Our duty as God's creatures is to obey His commandments unquestioningly."

The other approach is the sociological: "Values are not a matter of cosmic, but of social, order. They are necessary in any society for the protection of its members and for the smooth direction of its affairs. But human values exist only as matters of social convenience, and not because they are eternally right and true."

What about the first approach? Dogmatism is the first thing, certainly, to shun in any search for meaning. Dogmatism of any kind. For it is just as easy to be dogmatically *opposed* to religion as it is to be a religious fanatic.

It is quite as common, moreover, to find dogmatism in other spheres of thought as it is in religion. The reason dogmatism is so often associated with religion can be explained by a simple principle, which I've called the Law of Dogmatic Proliferation: *The dogmatic tendency increases in direct proportion to one's inability to prove a point.* This inability is greatest, certainly, in confrontation with the eternal mysteries.

What is needed now, however, is the clearest,

simplest, most honest approach possible. Religiously inclined people should be as honest in their approach as any skeptic. There is no evidence, indeed, to show that a sincere and open-minded search for truth has ever met with divine displeasure. Jesus Christ himself said, "The truth shall make you free."

More objective than the dogmatic approach so often associated with religion, and considerably more widely respected these days, is the approach taken by sociologists.

It is more or less generally accepted today that man is a social animal. Many of his most pressing problems do obviously revolve around his integration into the society in which he lives. It is also clear that men live together because in numbers they find greater security against want, greater strength to resist oppression, and greater opportunity to satisfy their normal need for emotional and intellectual stimulation. There is considerable ground, then, for the respect given this discipline.

Human conscience, according to the sociological approach, evolves entirely out of the demands that society makes on its individual members. Murder must be punished in the interests of communal safety. A cooperative spirit is appreciated because it benefits the group as a whole. Thus, man's sense of good and evil develops out of his endeavor to adapt himself to the communal code, and must be defined wholly in terms of this endeavor.

This approach is simple enough. It is down-to-earth enough. And it is unsentimental, thereby avoiding one of the main pitfalls on the path of any search for values. Why is it that, with these important points in its favor, it has not held its own against the swelling tide of mean-inglessness? Indeed, it has not done nearly so well in this regard as religious dogmatism. Why not?

The answer, simply, is that the sociological approach *is not concerned* with meaning. Indeed, in its entire emphasis on an ethic of democratic consent it only underscores life's essential meaninglessness.

There is also a basic fallacy in this approach. Approaching the subject quantitatively as it does, it overlooks the needs of the individual except insofar as these supplement the group's needs. But what are these needs, if not also the needs of its individual members?

The surest way to avoid vague thinking is to pin one's ideas to specific instances. J.W.N. Sullivan wrote, of the outlook of modern physics: "It is the electron that is the key to the universe." Similarly, it is man, the individual, who is the key to understanding society.

If the proper attitude of the individual were constantly to deny himself in favor of the group, and if every member of the group were taught to go at life in the same spirit, who, specifically, would end up being favored? It would be like the story of those two dignitaries about to ascend into a train, each bowing grandly to the other and exclaiming, "After *you,* Your Honor!" The train took off at last, leaving them fuming at each other on the station platform.

Group ethics makes the mistake of centering conscience, not in man, but—vaguely—in men. It is a shabby explanation, and shabbier still as a guideline, suggestive of that popular expression, "passing the buck." Accepted as a guideline, group ethics can permit wrong decisions too easily to be shrugged off as "their" responsibility. A ruthless leader can too easily step into such a picture and convince everyone that all this wonderful group spirit should be channeled toward the satisfaction of his own boundless ambitions.

That some sort of group ethics evolves in every civilization as a simple social necessity goes without saying. Obviously, there are rules and benefits that men seek in groups that they would not think of for themselves individually. Even in this case, however, the mainspring of action is the individual.

That the sociological approach is ultimately fallacious may be seen from the fact that large societies tend to be less conscientious than small ones. Institutionalism makes a parody of man's dreams of perfection. The more the individual is lost sight of in large masses of people, the greater the danger of finer perceptions being destroyed.

The Catholic Church has discovered this to be true, on a small scale, in its monastic orders. Small communities, it has found, tend more easily to preserve the Christian spirit. As the number of members grows, there is a marked tendency for this spirit to diminish. Petty rules and procedures begin to take precedence over spontaneous charity and cooperation. Individual needs are given diminishingly respectful attention. Individual conscience and initiative, whether spiritual or institutional, are increasingly discouraged as threats to the smooth functioning of the whole.

St. Teresa of Avila, familiar with these evils of the large monastery, stipulated that no community of her reformed Order of Discalced Carmelites might consist of more than eighteen nuns.

The over-systematization of large monastic communities is not an outgrowth of the monastic life as such. Institutionalism, not spiritual dedication, is the chain that binds personal conscience to the stone of uniformity. And institutionalism flourishes, weedlike, wherever large numbers of people are consolidated into social units.

Today, in an age of progressive consolidation at every level of society, private conscience is widely regarded with suspicion, even as a positive threat to the social order. Through overemphasis on institutionalism, the spirit of personal integrity seems well on its way to being lost; an amorphous idol of "togetherness" has been set up in its place. The new motto is not, "Think," but, "Agree!"

Because increasing systematization seems inevitable, it is growingly important to stress the truth that conscience is a personal, not a social, datum. Whether or not there is any way to escape the tightening grip of institutionalism on our shrinking world—in fact, especially if there be no escape from it—the individual must be looked to as never before to set the pace of moral and spiritual, as opposed to merely social, reforms. Man's worth as a man, and not merely as a social animal, must be deliberately enshrined, if only because the trend is so remorselessly to dehumanize him.

Systems abhor change. They represent an effort to freeze life's endless fluctuations into a still pose; to seal the bird of time in a timeless tomb.

Every advance in history, on the other hand, has come as a result of the crusading zeal of some one person—or perhaps of small groups of individuals, but of men and women who felt themselves stirred to their inner core by some great purpose or ideal. Great and uplifting changes have not emerged, except incidentally, from institutions. Great moral teachings have been accepted by mankind, not because of some legislative rule or admonishment, but because of the inspiration of a few great men and women. And the greatest teaching of the ages has ever been: "O man, seek strength and understanding *within* yourself!"

One cannot institutionalize originality. One cannot formulate rules to ensure creativity. One cannot legislate moral conviction.

Henry David Thoreau, in his classic essay *Civil Disobedience,* wrote: "I think we should be men first, and subjects afterward. It is not desirable to cultivate a respect for the law, so much as for the right. . . . Law never made men a whit more just; and, by means of their respect for it, even the well disposed are daily made the agents of injustice."

The question of ultimate values, in other words, should be liberated once and forever from the confining question of social conditioning. And while this liberation may cast us upon a sea of total uncertainty—loosing us as it does from all familiar traditions, cultural, social, and religious—we must accept the risk. Not to do so would be to cling to a dream that is fading in any case. An assumption of personal responsibility before the cosmic mysteries offers the only possible hope for a discovery of meaning in this age of moral, intellectual, and spiritual confusion.

There are two conceivable ways of assuming such personal responsibility. One would be to assume responsibility toward the great mysteries. The other would be a negative way. It would be to assume personal responsibility entirely toward oneself.

In later chapters we'll consider the first of these alternatives. In order to do so, however, it will be necessary to clear the terrain for it by examining the case for personal responsibility—not toward the universe, but in defiance of it.

CHAPTER THREE

Nihilism and the Search for Values

One hydrogen atom is a fair example of every other hydrogen atom. Is one man a fair example of every other man? Jean-Paul Sartre, the philosophical nihilist, claims that the answer to this question is, No. Every human being, he insists, is unique. A man's values, therefore, must be his own; no one else can decide questions of right and wrong for him.

Submitting Sartre's arguments to empirical scrutiny, we find that his theories simply do not fit the facts of life. Man's uniqueness is not radical; each person is only an expression of that universal phenomenon, mankind. In fact, by studying deeply the reasons for which an individual arrives at his own personal set of values, we find a basis for a value-system that is universal.

CHAPTER THREE

Nihilism and the Search for Values*

IF EVERYONE WERE to take it upon himself to seek his own values, might humanity soon find itself wandering in moral confusion?

Yes, perhaps, if such standards exist only by popular acclaim. But again, no, *if they exist already in the natural order.* Which of these alternatives is true? Are values only subjective? Or are they universal?

Western man tends to look upon human standards as inventions only—whether as time-honored social traditions, or as Godly whims that have been passed down to humanity as "commandments," but in either case not laws that are fundamental to Nature itself. Given this point of departure, one is bound to conclude that a few million declarations of personal values must indeed endanger the existing order, if only in the sense of challenging its coherence.

This conclusion has been reached, indeed, and quite without regret, by one of the most brilliant writers of

---

* The word *nihilism* is used here in the first sense given by Webster's dictionary: "A doctrine which denies any objective or real ground for truth. The doctrine which denies any objective ground for moral principles."

our times, Jean-Paul Sartre. Sartre, whether one likes him or not, cannot be safely overlooked in any modern search for meaning. He is a nihilist, but his nihilism is a logical consequence of the growing realization of our age that values cannot be institutionalized, and that they *must* therefore be sought on a personal level.

Sartre at least has had the integrity to mince no words on the point. His nihilism is almost a creative affirmation. He announces calmly that if a person really chooses, of his own free will, to rape, plunder, or kill, he should pursue these resolutions as if his salvation depended on it.

Orestes, the hero of his three-act drama, *The Flies,* kills his own mother, Clytemnestra, then rhapsodizes: "I am free . . . Free. And at one with myself." Later he cries: "You see me, men of Argos, you understand that my crime is wholly mine; I claim it as my own, for all to know; it is my glory, my life's work."

In *Saint Genet,* a biographical sketch, Sartre praises as the ideal existentialist—as, indeed, a true and living *saint*—a poet who totally accepted his identity as a criminal—who had the glowing "integrity," in fact, not merely to write about thieves and male prostitutes, but to be both of these himself.

Sartre gives us, as examples of self-integrated human beings, men who chose deliberately—that is, without any outside pressure, obligation, or necessity of any kind—to act as they did. This freedom of choice is the central point of his philosophy.

The theme is not without noble antecedents. Many of the great men of history have stressed freedom, too.

They have insisted, for example, on strengthening the will to resist false guidance. They have harped constantly on the importance of freeing human conscience from mere questions of social convention.

To Sartre, however, who believes in no objective truth, freedom means *any* act of the will that is uninfluenced by extraneous factors. As he puts it: "One may choose anything if it is on the grounds of free involvement."*

May one, however, choose literally *anything?* And can one be perfectly sure that such a choice will be "on the grounds of free involvement"?

Supposing one were to choose, by a deliberate act of free will, to take heroin daily? Many persons have done so, and have fancied that in their choice they were free. The time came, however—such is heroin's power—when they were no longer free men, but slaves, gripped by a vice that tyrannized over them and finally destroyed them.

Sartre argues that man is "radically" free because he always has the choice to accept or reject. Once the heroin habit is formed, however, the freedom to reject it is hardly "radical." Often, it is entirely absent.

Well, but was there "radical" freedom at least in the initial decision to take heroin? How could there have been? Such a choice would be determined, surely, by previous habit patterns. For let us ask ourselves this question: Can any man, as a deliberate affirmation of his freedom, commit himself *knowingly* into bondage? Isn't the very query absurd? Freedom abhors bondage. A man

---

* *Existentialism,* translated by Bernard Frechtman (New York, Philosophical Library, 1947), p. 57.

affirms his freedom for the sake of prolonging it, or—better still—of increasing it, but never for the sake of losing it. As Sartre himself states: "Freedom in every concrete circumstance can have no other aim than to want itself."* If a man enslaves himself willingly, without pressure of necessity of any kind, it simply means that he has failed to appreciate the consequences of his act. In fact, he is already bound by his own ignorance, because of which bondage he willingly—though unknowingly—commits himself to still greater bondage.

The same holds true for actions far more innocuous than taking heroin. The "freedom" of any sense indulgence is experienced only so long as one consents to it. Let anyone try to stop such an indulgence—especially one of many year's standing—and he'll quickly realize how very much a captive he is. It is easy enough to roll a stone downhill; it is not so easy to heave it back up the hill again. Actions, many times repeated, turn into habits, and habits are as difficult to shake off as hungry creditors. Mark Twain put it well in his wry boast: "Smoking is the easiest habit in the world to give up; I've done it a thousand times."

If, therefore, radical freedom is defined as mere license to do anything one chooses, with no consideration for the consequences of one's choice, one must conclude that this definition is idealistic, perhaps, but not realistic. If it is admitted, moreover, that *any* action could prove harmful *in itself,* one discovers at once a basis for a universal code of morals. *For if specific actions lead necessarily to specific results, this means that*

* Ibid., p. 53.

certain values, at least, do exist independently of any human invention or consent.

Sartre insists that man's freedom exiles him from Nature, and that *therefore* man is not subject to its laws nor bound by any natural consequences. But here his reasoning becomes shoddy. Obviously, man's freedom from Nature *depends on* whether or not he is subject to Nature's laws. To make his freedom the premise, and his non-subjection the deduction from that premise, is like trying to fly a flag before erecting the flagpole. It is not a reasonable argument.

And here we observe an interesting facet of Sartre's writings, one that it would be well to point out in passing because it marks a tendency so common to Western philosophy: the tendency to bend facts to fit some preconceived theory, instead of basing theory on an initial observation of the facts. The result is very often unfortunate. Where the process is deliberate, it can only be termed deliberately dishonest.

The great merit of Sartre's writings is that he spells out his meanings so clearly. His willingness to put his theories ruthlessly into practice makes it possible also the more easily to test their validity. But the reader must be warned that Sartre himself is not interested in making any such test. Indeed, one cannot but wonder whether his defection from this duty is not conscious and deliberate.

For Sartre, like many brilliant men, seems to be quite willing to substitute brilliance for integrity. In his play, *Nekrassov,* he betrays his delight in "proving" the impossible. The hero of this eight-scene "farce" is

Georges de Valera, a confidence man and a perfect genius in persuasion. Posing as the Russian defector Nekrassov, Georges succeeds in convincing an acquaintance who has known him for years that this familiarity is a hallucination, and that, definite knowledge to the contrary notwithstanding, he really is Nekrassov.

Sartre, too, appears to be a sort of confidence man—a con man of philosophy. He uses brilliant arguments to plead notions that everyone knows to be absurd. Yet, despite their knowledge, many people—brilliant people like himself, intellectuals who appreciate a subtle argument—first accept his philosophy as interesting, and later defend it as true.

Sartre was a brilliant man. Reality, however, cannot be played with like a toy. The greatest genius cannot make a falsehood true.

We have already seen that certain actions—such as taking heroin—cannot but bind and enslave the will. Sartre underscores his teaching on man's utter freedom of choice by saying that Nature does not compel us to do anything. We are not forced, in other words, to eat. If we choose, we can always abstain from food and starve ourselves to death. Some choice!

In itself, his reasoning is absurd. In a game of cards, one's freedom of choice involves the cards he may play, and not the question of whether he may shoot himself, or tear up the cards and overturn the card table in a fit of temper. It is begging the question to say that our freedom in the game of life is absolute because we can always chuck the game. The question of freedom concerns our position *in* the game, not *out* of it. Nor (if one considers the teaching of all the great religions) is it by any means certain that we shall escape the consequences of our acts by merely dying.

Sartre's statement is not convincing. It does, however, underscore an important point: Short of the drastic "solution" of deliberate self-starvation—that is to say, if we want to stay alive—Nature *does* compel us to eat. Looking further, we see that if we want to adopt an inadequate diet, we can do so if we like, but we cannot thereby avoid the consequences: We shall remain undernourished, without energy, listless. If we want to eat only rich foods, again, we are perfectly free to fulfill our desire, but eventually we shall pay the penalty of disease.

The conclusion is obvious: Whatever efforts be made to prove that there are no *absolute* values, or that invention plays a role in man's search for social and religious values, it cannot honestly be said that there are no natural values at all. There are certain facts of nature with which we simply have to harmonize ourselves or else pay the unpleasant consequences.

This truth is self-evident. Yet, so conditioned are people by modern science to the idea of *mastering* Nature that they often imagine that there is no fact of Nature which man cannot, eventually, bend to his own purposes. One tends to forget that it is only by *cooperating* with Nature that we can get her to serve us at all. We do not invent her laws; we merely discover them and put them to use.

The kind of choice with which Sartre presents us is not the crucial one. The true issue, from a practical moral standpoint, is not so much whether we have the power to choose, but rather whether, according to natural law, there are not *right* choices and *wrong* ones. Evidently, there are rules to the game of life, and if we want to win the game the first thing we must do is learn what the rules are, and abide by them.

"But in that case," some fan of Sartre's may object, "we are all slaves! Freedom is only a myth, if the opportunity to choose is burdened with penalties for every choice but the right one."

In a sense this is true. Man's freedom cannot be absolute so long as he is bound by natural law. But words can be tricky playthings. One often thinks of the free man, morally speaking, as a libertine; one imagines freedom to mean unbridled indulgence in any vice. Such a concept is seen to be fallacious once it is realized that *wrong* actions actually lead one into greater bondage. Freedom, as Sartre himself has said, can have no other aim than to want itself. Thus, the longing for freedom, rightly understood, will in itself prevent one from going against the lawful demands of nature, which offer man the only assurance of freedom that he has.

If we persist in eating wrongly, we'll ultimately destroy our health, our happiness, and our vitality. Becoming a prey to disease, our strength vitiated by constant fatigue, we shall find our will more and more enslaved to the oppressive demands of the body.

If, on the other hand, we eat rightly, we find that our bodies will obey us as we want them to. If there is something that we'd like to do, the chances are we'll find the strength to do it. We'll be able to arise when we want to, sleep when we want to, run, dance, work hard, as we choose. The better we cooperate with the way our bodies are actually made, instead of pretending unrealistically that they are somehow made differently, the better we can free ourselves of their most arrogant imperatives.

The very instinct for freedom causes us to choose those actions which give us freedom, rather than any that will enslave us. If we act against that freedom, it is because we do not clearly understand the nature of our actions, or else because previous wrong actions have already enmeshed us in harmful habits.

Freedom, applied freely and knowingly, can only choose the path of law, which is to say, the path of reality. The choice is similar to that faced by a chauffeur, who knows that, while it may be possible to steer his car from a variety of positions, it steers best from the driver's seat.

Thus, we find at least some basis for a claim that objective values already exist in the natural order. But how do these principles apply to the examples Sartre gives us of freedom on a moral, as opposed to a merely physical, level?

Let us compare his Orestes to life itself as we know it, and ask ourselves whether it would really be possible for a human being to commit some unspeakable atrocity—to kill his own mother, say—and to exult afterward: "I am free! I am at one with myself!"

One example should suffice: Joseph Stalin. He doesn't fit the bill perfectly, of course. For one thing, he appears to have suffered none of the exquisite ordeal of self-analysis through which Sartre's heroes are obliged to put themselves. Still, with a minimum of rationalization he arrived at many of the same conclusions. Again, unlike them, he took care not to shout to the world that he was a crook. But to his co-workers, at least, he seems to have been frank enough about his activities. And although he was a communist and therefore, supposedly, a determined foe of existential individualism, in fact he was only as communistic as he needed to be to further his own ambitions. He may not have believed in individualism where others were concerned, but he certainly believed in it wholeheartedly for himself.

To Stalin, the welfare or suffering of the people as a whole, which should have been his concern both as a communist and as the ruler of his people, meant nothing at all. In this he differed from Orestes not a bit: Both men talked of love while they killed. If the populace opposed Stalin, he was perfectly capable, as he demonstrated with a vengeance in the Ukraine, of causing millions to perish. When his own wife died, he mourned her demise as a tragedy. But of the death of millions, brought about by himself, he remarked calmly that these were merely a "statistic." Political opponents were ruthlessly exterminated by him. In the 1930s he conducted a blood purge of countless officials because he feared a take-over by a mere handful of subordinates.

He worshiped no God but himself. Frequently, as he rode in a car through the streets of Moscow, he would repeat, "I am stalin! I am steel! I am steel!" Complete, ruthless power over himself as well as over everyone else: This was his creed, his only goal. It was not a *passion,* mind you; Stalin was not a passionate man. Cold, hard, and remorseless to the core, he was a spartan of self-control whose every act was as deliberate and as pitiless as anything Sartre could imagine. His entire life was of his own making, a true expression of the ideal that Sartre has described.

He was the dictator of the largest country in the world. No one dared to challenge his authority. Surely he, of all men, was in a position to declare convincingly with Orestes: "I am free!"

But he was not free. He was a slave of countless fears and suspicions. Conscience, in the sense of remorse at having flouted the established moral order, bothered him not at all. He had no rules but his own. He cared not for the judgments of man or God. His fears, even as his achievements, were entirely of his own making. And they were obsessive.

He trusted nobody. In his own view, the people whom he had downtrodden had only one desire: his downfall; the subordinates whom he ruled with an iron fist had only one ambition: to strike back as pitilessly at him. His closest associates were the objects of his darkest distrust. As he had dealt fairly with no man, so he was incapable of imagining fairness, sincerity, or goodwill to be genuinely a part of any man's nature. Where other people may enjoy the confidence of friends, and the security of a world that entertains no wish to betray them, Stalin was alone in a self-projected world of enemies, some of them self-conceived, and others of them actually created by his actions against them. Where other men can relax comfortably in their homes or in public, and can sleep undisturbed at night in their beds,

Stalin could relax never. Always he was steeled to meet his foes, lest they spring on him unawares.

His isolation from others was at first a matter of choice. Later, it became as much a terrified instinct for survival.

Lucky man! So his rivals may indeed have imagined him. He had everything he had ever worked for: power, position, fame, unlimited freedom to do exactly as he willed. And yet—strange is the balance of justice!—he was enmeshed in a form of slavery the enormity of which few men can even conceive. Miserable wretch! Only a madman, glimpsing even from afar the ceaseless torments that were his in his unchallenged dominion, could want to exchange places with him for a mere half-hour!

But see now the meaning of this history. Here was a man who bowed to no God, who honored no laws, who scorned the most time-honored traditions of men. He had no values but his own, those which suited his own convenience. He was completely lacking in what most men would call a conscience. If moral values were purely man-made, he should have been a shining ruler, even—by Sartre's standards—a saint. He was neither.

Something *in his own nature* cast a cloud over what ought, if Sartre's philosophy had any merit at all, to have been a rare and joyous fulfillment. Something tore into shreds of insecurity and worry what ought, if values were merely personal, to have been the soothing mantle of perfection. In his life he tasted none of the sweetness of heaven, but he suffered more than his share of the agonies of hell.

Is it really possible for men to create their own

moral values arbitrarily? Just see how determinedly Stalin tried to do so. And mark how colossally he failed. Does it not appear that there were facts of his own nature which, like the laws of physics, demanded recognition—to serve him if he lived by them, but to destroy him if he worked against them?

Stalin's life was an example of a simple, universal fact of human nature: If a person acts to hurt others, or if he sets himself in determined opposition to the world, he will automatically—indeed, *necessarily*—steel himself to receive its opposition in return. Forever tensed (since he knows not when the opposition may strike), unable to find even a moment's trusting peace, such a person may well end up in a mental institution. That Stalin did not meet such an end (though there are reports that he went mad toward the end) may be a tribute to his strength, but not to his inner freedom.

What, then, of freedom? Is not tension a form of psychological bondage? Yes, and of the cruelest sort, too. By comparison with it, even a man in a dungeon may feel himself relatively free. Any man who dwells on constant thoughts of opposition, destruction, or tyranny will live in a state of unceasing tension. It cannot be otherwise. How can such a man know the sweetness of true freedom?

"But wait!" the Sartre apologist may cry. "What about the person who *enjoys* danger, who delights as much in being opposed by others as he does in opposing them? What about the warlike hero? the prize fighter? the daredevil courting danger just for the thrill of it?

Doesn't the very enjoyment of such people prove them, in the sense you imply, to be free?"

But my friend, here you raise no contradiction. We have spoken of deliberate oppression. People may fancy they enjoy a little competition, or a few searing hazards to enliven their monotonous lives. They may fight nobly for an ideal and sleep thereafter the sleep of the virtuous. But let malevolence once breathe upon them in their games—let them just feel the will to use other men for their own ends, the wish to harm or destroy for selfish gain—and soon, very soon will their enjoyment become rusted over. Let such monstrous intentions grow and seize possession of their personalities, becoming their boon companions, and any honest joys they may have known in life will become for them only dreams. Why ask of the hereafter? Hell, not heaven, will be their lot right here on earth.

One could hardly find a better example of genuine ruthlessness than Joseph Stalin. But in other cases—in tyrants like Adolf Hitler, in the gangster "warlords" of our times, in the Machiavellian schemers that litter the pages of history—we find the same insidious malaise. It is inevitable. What we are, that we shall imagine others to be also. As we treat them, so we must expect them at least to *want* to treat us in return. The man of ruthless ambition can never relax trustfully. The very walls will seem to menace him. Should he live his entire life out unmolested, he will nevertheless be a slave, trapped in a dungeon of his own brooding creation.

And so, too, for other crimes.

Anyone who makes his living by thievery, for example,

will have more to deal with than an outraged society. He may be amoral to the core, perturbed not at all that he is behaving in a way that others consider wrong. But he punishes himself nonetheless.

The person who makes money honestly may feel some natural concern for its protection. But, being honest himself, he is at least not likely to imagine that all the world wants to rob him of what is rightfully his.

The thief, on the other hand, has a triple fear: the normal concern of ownership; the knowledge that what he has taken is not rightfully his, and that it is therefore in constant danger of being reclaimed from him; and, since he sees the world with the consciousness of a thief, the suspicion that the world is full of people who *want* to rob him, lawfully or unlawfully, of all that he owns.

The thief does not merely own his possessions. He is possessed by them. He is their slave, and his every new theft places yet another bar in a cage of his own making, a cage within which he shuts himself off from the world. This is no comfortable den into which he might withdraw cozily after a day's honest labor. It is a prison from which he will be able to find no escape— none, at least, so long as he remains a thief.

One of the most natural impulses in life is toward self-expansion. All creatures reach out for new experiences, new knowledge, broader identifications. To reverse this trend by a deliberate act of will, to contract one's little self into a still-more-shriveled littleness— this is, clearly, not merely to restrict, but with the restriction to invite pain. The thief, by taking from others for his own selfish gain, thinks to expand his dominion by adding to his possessions. But in fact he confines himself; gradually, he grows narrow, mean, jealous, and suspicious of the intentions of others. Even the increase of his property results in a shrinking of his actual dominion, and with the shrinking he experiences pain.

"It is more blessed to give than to receive." So taught Jesus Christ. More blessed indeed, for giving is self-expansive, and liberating. It creates joy in the giver. The generous heart beholds a trusting, not a hostile, world.

No, even in Sartre—perhaps especially in Sartre, since his unequivocal dependence on *created* values brings the issue so sharply in focus—we see that human values are not arbitrary. People, and societies, may indeed invent their own social codes. There are facts of Nature, however, that await no man's approval. If man ignores those facts, he suffers. If whole societies turn against them, then whole societies must bear the painful consequences.

Using Sartre as our point of departure, then, we have found that moral values cannot be voted into or out of existence by popular acclaim. Nor are they only "commandments," arbitrarily given by the Deity, but to be obeyed nevertheless by an uncomprehending and reluctant humanity in defiance of its every natural instinct. They are, rather, guidelines to certain laws that govern our own nature—objective safeguards, worth knowing if we want to avoid having to learn every lesson in life the hard way.

CHAPTER FOUR

Values—Absolute, or Relative?

Science tells us that everything is relative. Many people nowadays have made this teaching an excuse for moral irresponsibility. "If I steal"—so goes their reasoning— "you may lose something, but I shall be the gainer. From my own standpoint, I'll have done a good thing. Everything, you see, is relative!"

Relativity is so often summoned up to support a doctrine of meaninglessness that concerned thinkers have tended to condemn relativity along with nihilism itself. Their commitment to moral absolutism, however, merely affirms the widening communication-gap between traditional thinking and the revolutionary insights of modern science. It is as if aristocrats, on hearing reports of a popular uprising, were to remark: "There is no cause for a revolution; therefore, there is no revolution." Relativity cannot be so lightly dismissed.

In this chapter we'll study the classic defense of moral absolutism that was made by Immanuel Kant, and conclude that absolutism is untenable nowadays as a moral philosophy.

CHAPTER FOUR

Values—Absolute, or Relative?

A BOY FROM A WELL-TO-DO HOME is caught stealing from a local store. The crime sits lightly on his conscience. Asked if he doesn't think it wrong to steal, he replies with a shrug: "Everything is relative."

Crime is becoming commonplace; the boy's answer, even more so. "Everything is relative." One hears the expression everywhere these days. Implicit in it is the belief that, since all is relative, everything one does must be meaningless anyway, so—why not do as one pleases?

Relativity is a fact of nature. Yet law also is a fact of nature. Moreover, as we saw in the last chapter, there are laws governing human nature that impel us human beings toward right behavior. If a person eats wrongly, his health will suffer. And if he exercises properly, he is more likely to remain in exuberant good health.

In ethical philosophy, relativity translates as relativism. And relativism, despite erudite attempts to clothe it in dignity, translates popularly as a rationale for amoral behavior. If, however, both relativity and some kind of moral law form part of the natural order, they cannot be divorced from each other. There is a point to remember, also, about the natural order: It accepts no excuses. There is no point, in other words, in crying, when the time comes to pay up, "But I didn't know any better!"

In the chapters to come we shall see that moral law not only exists as part of the relative natural order, but offers at the same time the kind of lofty guidelines that civilized man naturally expects. In this chapter, however, we must approach the subject from the other end of the scale, with the more traditional view of morality.

Intrinsic in our Western heritage has been the assumption that moral values are absolute. If this is what they really are, then they must be not only above life's relativities, but above natural law as well.

Probably the best defense ever made of moral absolutism was that of the great German philosopher, Immanuel Kant.

Kant emphasized, first, the fallacy of looking outside oneself for moral guidelines. The lack of certainty in the results of any action makes it impossible, he said, to look to those results for absolutes. (His argument, it may be noted, is predicated on the *a priori* assumption that, for moral standards to be valid, they must also be absolute.)

Nothing could be more acceptable than the fact that matters do not always turn out as our sense of justice dictates they should. The results of action are forever unpredictable, the most well intentioned deed having sometimes disastrous consequences. A generous gift may become instrumental in corrupting its recipients. An innocent offer of help may unsuspectingly aid a crime. On this point, then, Kant was obviously right: Any search for *fixed* standards of behavior certainly cannot begin with a study of the consequences of action. These must be ruled out from the start.

Where, then, to look?

We must, Kant insisted, look upward to our principles, to our original motives.

Kant reasoned that if a person's motives are right, his deeds, morally speaking, will be right also, *regardless of their final outcome.* Kant based his thesis on what he called the "categorical imperative"—a moral principle, inwardly recognized by every man, which all men are conscience-bound to obey.

Moral values exist, as we have ascertained already in our study of the effect of generosity *on the people themselves* who are generous. The question is, are those values absolute? Are moral principles forever fixed and unbending? Are they under all circumstances necessarily and *equally* true?

The answer to all three of these questions would have, from a point of view of relativity, to be, No. For one thing, people in their actual behavior often find themselves faced with a choice between two or more conflicting principles. For them at such times, one "imperative" necessarily becomes more "categorical" than another.

Consider an example:

Both truthfulness and charity must certainly be classed as Kantian categorical imperatives. To call a dull-witted man stupid, however, would be uncharitable, however true the statement. One "imperative," in other words, would need to be compromised to make room for the other. By tactful silence, for example—even, if pressed for a verdict, by cautious equivocation—truthfulness might have to defer to charity.

Yet one couldn't say therefore that, of the two principles, charity is the more imperative. Indeed, even to suggest a relativity of imperatives would be to call their absoluteness into question. But there are other times when charity must step aside for truthfulness—situations, for example, when the magnitude of an issue overshadows any merely personal consideration.

Mountain air may be pure, but when it drifts into the cities with their car and bus fumes, their smoke, their panting hordes of humanity, the air's purity very quickly becomes polluted. Absolute principles, similarly, when dragged down into the work-a-day world, cannot but be polluted by the world's relativities.

Applications of a principle are not the same thing as the principle itself, any more than a ray of sunlight piercing the clouds is the same thing as the sun itself. They are limited expressions, merely, of the actual principle.

The very concepts we form of that principle can only *represent* the actual principle; they cannot equal it. Whether or not the truth they represent is absolute, their representation of it will necessarily be only partial, and cannot therefore do it anything but relative justice. The gulf between infinity and finitude is infinity itself. And the gulf, similarly, between absolute and relative truth is itself absolute.

This, then, is a serious defect in Kant's reasoning: He makes his *a priori* assumption of fixed values itself a "categorical imperative." Any specific principles he subsequently attaches to that assumption are not more imperative than the assumption itself; indeed, they derive their categorical status from it. In imposing them, however, in all their unqualified finality on this realm of relativity, his reasoning runs into difficulties. For when principles are applied, they must also be interpreted. By interpretation, moreover, they necessarily become subject to relativity's inconsistencies.

Kant's only means of saving moral principles from the pollutions of relativism is to screen them off from their actional effects. These, as he says, are always uncertain. What he fails to observe is that absolute principles enter the realm of relativity long before they reach those effects.

When a meteor enters the earth's atmosphere, it is transformed by it. If it is not large enough to survive the heat of its descent, it is consumed altogether. The same may be said of abstract principles. As they enter the human mind, and indeed by the very fact of being perceived by the mind, they are transformed. The denser the mental "atmosphere" of an individual's egotism, dullness, and desires, the greater the likelihood of their essential truth vanishing altogether.

For practical purposes, we may describe the levels of descent as follows:

First, there is the individual's *understanding* of a principle. This, already, is a diminution of the principle itself.

Second, there is the individual's rational *interpretation* of his more or less intuitive understanding.

Third, there are the *intentions* that he forms on the basis of that interpretation, in which the interpretation itself can never be completely represented.

Fourth, there are the *actions,* proceeding from, but never fully representing, those intentions.

Only at this stage do we arrive at the consequences of action, which to Kant's mind posed the sole obstacle to moral absolutism. In truth, as we have seen, it is not possible for the human mind to think in absolute terms, enmeshed as mankind is in the consciousness of relativities.

Each stage in the conception and manifestation of a principle is a step downward into relativity, and away from its original source in whatever absolutes there be.

Consider for a moment the third of these stages: the intention. I may intend to give money to a widow. Perhaps my causal principle is charity, which I may understand as kindness, and interpret further to mean the doing of good deeds. One particular intention, however, cannot express in its *entirety* the interpretation that I place on the word "kindness." Nor can I condense into mere dollar bills my feelings of good will for the poor widow, my anxiety to relieve her suffering, my wish to give her peace of mind and happiness. These intangibles will be only symbolized by my gift. A symbol, too, cannot equal the reality that it represents.

Charity, however absolute in its origins, becomes diminished at the very outset of its descent into human consciousness. For we may understand charity as kindness, but it is much more than that. And we may interpret kindness as the doing of good deeds, but kindness, too, is much more than good deeds.

Kant believed that reason, based on absolute moral principles, would ensure the absolute moral correctness of any action. He was mistaken. Not only is it impossible for any action to be *absolutely* correct. The intention behind the action, indeed the very initial understanding of the underlying principle itself, cannot but be flawed.

This discussion, however, would be but a quibble, and there would be no harm in moral absolutism at all, if it really inspired people always to live by high principles. The trouble is that human understanding is too often clouded by desire, egotism, ignorance, or sheer stupidity. Too often has moral absolutism, dogmatically blind to all relative considerations, been responsible even for the most atrocious crimes.

Consider an ethico-religious value that is, surely, a categorical imperative if any be such: the service of God. Here is an ideal that has inspired some of the noblest deeds in history. To serve God, men and women have sacrificed their comfort, their security, their health, their very lives. Yet for the sake of this ideal, also, brutal wars have been fought, and countless atrocities committed. One thinks of the Spanish Inquisition, when church leaders ruthlessly tortured people—heretics and innocent alike—and burned them at the stake in the name of God, Whom in their daily prayers they were obligated to address as the God of Love.

Must we denounce all those churchmen as *deliberately* evil? It is far more likely that some of them, at least, were sincere in their religion. But they saw the welfare of the Church as necessary for the spread of untold good on earth. They must, moreover, have believed—abstractly at least—in the love of Christ, and in the need of mankind for that love. It can only have been to defend true spiritual ideals that the best of them tried to stamp out what they saw as the spreading fires of schism and heresy. Their underlying principles, in this case, were unassailable. But their application of those principles can only be described as monstrous, even demonic.

How was it possible for religiously minded men to imagine that God could be served by such ungodly acts? Only one answer suggests itself: They subscribed to the same error into which Kant later fell so readily. They believed in the absoluteness of right and wrong in this relative world. Convinced *a priori* that the authority of the Church was an absolute good, they necessarily persuaded themselves that any challenge to that authority constituted a threat, and must therefore be interpreted as absolutely evil and wrong.

No objective test of this conviction struck them as being necessary. The fact that persecution, torture, and murder are themselves offenses against the most fundamental teachings of Christianity formed no part of their neatly framed picture. They didn't look upon their executions as *murder*. They considered themselves the champions of good. Whatever means they used in defense of their convictions were to them, therefore, inconsequential. The absoluteness of their convictions demanded a corresponding absoluteness in their

propagation and defense. There were for them no qualifying clauses to be inserted into the pact they felt they
had made with God. The Lord must triumph: Satan
must be destroyed. Before the towering grandeur of this
cosmic drama, the pains and sufferings of mere mortals
were of absolutely no consequence.

Kant did not invent absolutism. It was part and
parcel of his Western heritage, too familiar to him to
awaken his distrust.

It is only the discoveries of Twentieth-Century science that, with their revelations of the relativity of time,
space, size, force, motion, and of practically everything
else in the universe, have begun to undermine Western
man's faith also in the existence of absolute human
values. Kant was born too early to be exposed to these
ideas. He accepted moral absolutism without question.
It is a credit to his genius that he was able to give his
ethical preconceptions such ponderous support.

His one-sided endeavor, however, to justify actions
and intentions by referring them solely to their underlying principles was unrealistic. Unnoticed by him, it
opened the door to almost as adamant a philosophy of
nihilism. Kant tried valiantly to revive the cause of moral
virtue, yet the very arguments be used became the premise
from which Jean-Paul Sartre—to cite a prime example—
was able to draw diametrically opposite conclusions.

Kant's stress on *a priori* truths (truths that require
no empirical verification because their intrinsic and
absolute existence has already been revealed by reason)
made it possible for Sartre to claim the same justification
for his own completely nihilistic approach to values.

Kant's effort to establish an absolute moral order by discounting the effects of morality in the realm of action made it possible for Sartre, following Kant's respected example, to justify an utterly preposterous ethic, opposed to all moral experience, yet solemnly haloed in philosophical tradition.

Theoretical reason may follow a neat and orderly line if we carefully shield it from all practical consequences, with their inconveniently qualifying *if*s, *maybe*s, and *but*s. But reason may be neat and orderly without necessarily being right. (Where did the expression come from: "Devilishly ingenious, but damnably wrong"?) Logic, to be realistic, *must* take into account objective facts and consequences. The most abstract principles need to be tested against concrete evidence. For such practical experimentation neither Sartre nor Kant made any provision.

Kant summed up his ethic with these famous words of advice: "Act as if the principle on which your action is based were to become by your will a universal law of nature." If absolutism were valid, this would be a noble call to moral vigor, indeed! Kant's one-sided concentration on cause, however, in utter disregard of effect, blinded him to the danger that someone, acting on his advice, might strive vigorously to impose his *errors* on others, to make his every mistake "a universal law of nature."* And if mere errors can be so perpetuated, why

---

* Kant's dictum contains an even greater fallacy, one that contradicts his own philosophy of the *preexistence* of absolute principles. For if one acts on such a principle, surely it is *already* a "universal law of nature." How then can one's actions *make* that principle into a law?

not evils too—and with self-righteous determination, in the name of truth?

The earlier inquisitors, had they thought of it, might have written Kant's dictum for him; they certainly lived by it conscientiously enough. Sartre did think of it, having Kant's philosophy before him as a model. It was no Herculean labor for him to enlist Kant's teaching in support of his own vigorous, quasi-moralistic brand of nihilism.

Communism, too, has thrived on the expression of this sort of absolutist moral vigor. Communists baldly claim that a truth is any statement that advances the communist cause, and a lie, anything that obstructs it. Karl Marx was a philosophical heir, through Hegel, to the absolutism of Kant.

Consider for a moment the infamous dictum: "The end justifies the means." An end might, of course, be rightly said to justify the means if we were to speak of the end as an accomplished fact, and not as a merely tentative expectation. As Jesus put it, "By their fruits ye shall know them." (Matthew 7:20) By "end," however, in this context, is usually meant some goal that one has only in his mind, without having as yet demonstrated its validity. History has amply shown the fallacy of such theoretical "justifications." Without the acid test of actual outcome—relative and imperfect though this test, too, must certainly be—it is easy to apply oneself with complete self-righteousness to the wrong means entirely.

Communist workers are notorious for doing just that. The ruthless tactics they employ have never achieved the peaceful ends they proclaim. Theory to them, however, is all-sufficient. The consistent failure of their theoretical system in the field of practical action is not, in their eyes, even worthy of notice. They are absolutists. Intent on achieving some eventual, to them absolute, good, because they view their theories as categorical imperatives, they justify the brutal means they employ by pointing with confidence to their as-yet-unproved hypotheses.

Only absolutism can permit such utter self-deception.

What hope, then, for a clear-cut moral order? Does the fact that human values are, and cannot but be, relative return us with reinforced conviction to the doubt raised in Chapter One that no values exist, and that life is, as so many people claim, meaningless?

Not necessarily. It only shows that the justifications that have been made for morality so far have been unrealistic. There is no need to conclude from this fact that no basis for morality exists.

Rigidity in one's moral view, as we have seen, actually makes a person less moral, not more so. The extremes of self-righteousness which this view permits will often blind people to natural charity. In the past, such self-righteousness has made possible the inquisitions, the witch-burnings, the "white-man's-burden" consciousness, and the intolerance of countless other shades that is relatively unknown wherever absolutism holds less powerful sway.

It was with high-sounding slogans and lofty ideals that Robespierre—considered by many to have been a genuine idealist—advanced to the forefront of the Reign of Terror during the French Revolution. Kant, gentle philosopher though he was, hailed that revolution with unmitigated joy, remaining apparently indifferent to the sufferings of thousands of innocent people. So also have many politicians enhaloed heinous deeds in pious maxims; religious organizations, self-righteously encompassed the ruin of innocent individuals; and men and women everywhere, given selfish cruelty the weight of a divine decree.

Absolutism corrupts the very ideal of perfection. If a mountain is known to rise high above our familiar foothills, some of us may be inspired to set out and conquer it. But if we are persuaded that these homely hillocks of ours are "absolutely" high—or as high, at any rate, as mountains can possibly rise—how many people will take the trouble to seek greater heights to conquer? Worse still, since these foothills of ours offer no real challenge anyway, it may turn out that no one will bother to climb even them.

Our moral pace-setters, having determined that theirs is the sacred right of final judgment in these matters, pass on to the rest of us their very human notions of what perfection means. Cosmic "absolutes" are cut down by such petty minds to very little mounds, and everyone finds sufficient incentive to remain exactly as he is.

If we are going to search for meaning in life, the first thing we must do is face frankly the fact that relativities do exist, and therefore cannot safely be ignored. Values must be seen as ultimate goals—absolute, possibly, somewhere in outer space, but certainly not here on solid earth. In the realm of daily, practical living, they must be accepted in all their bewildering relativity.

Right and wrong need to be considered not as abstractions, merely, but in the actual context of specific acts, of specific situations.

We shall see, in the next chapter, that the farther a line of reasoning gets away from its source, the greater becomes the possibility for error. The same is true, as we have seen in this chapter, of morality.

It is not enough for a person to adhere to high ideals. His application of those ideals must be checked also, to see how truly he expresses them in action. For values in action cannot be anything but relatively valid. Recognition of this fact is a reminder, if nothing else, of the need for careful, constant checking.

CHAPTER FIVE

Truth Is Not Reasonable!

Traditionally, Western philosophical and religious thinking has tried to set reality, and therefore moral values, firmly, as if in concrete. Modern science has discovered the universe to be not fixed, but endlessly fluid. Western thinkers have concluded, consequently, that, in the absence of absolute values, the universe, and therefore human life, are essentially meaningless. A few thinkers, of course, with Sartre, have gleefully proclaimed meaninglessness as the new "meaning" of life. In no case, however, has Western philosophy really been able to adapt itself convincingly to the deep philosophical implications inherent in the discoveries of modern science.

For modern science has all but abandoned rationalism. Western civilization, on the other hand, is rooted in rationalism. If we are to cope with this newly unfamiliar universe of fluid relativities, it is essential that new ways of thinking be explored.

Truth Is Not Reasonable!

IN THIS BOOK we are concerned with the conviction, widespread in this Twentieth Century, that the universe is essentially meaningless, and that human life is devoid of ultimate purpose. This conviction, as we saw in Chapter One, is the result of new findings in science that seem to contradict traditional notions of right and wrong, of justice and injustice.

Approaching the question of moral values from a standpoint of natural law, we have found that certain facts of human nature do support the reality of what we call moral values. But we have also found that these values cannot rightly be considered absolutes, for they must submit, along with everything else in the universe, to the vagaries of relativity.

To many readers, it must seem that we have argued ourselves into a circle. For it is precisely because values do seem to be relative that so many thinking people have concluded that values either do not exist, or are simply not definitive enough to be binding on human behavior. It is common today to view moral principles as myths agreed upon. In the past, the way to "fight the good fight" for truth has always been to strike blows for absolutism. And here we are, claiming that truth is not necessarily undermined by relativity. How can such contradictions exist? The answer, as we shall see, lies in a reinterpetation of relativity as it applies to human affairs.

Fundamental to the problem of meaninglessness is the Western notion that the universe must either be ruled by rational principles or else be totally irrational. Western civilization is rooted in the conviction that, for anything to be meaningful, it must also be understandable in rational terms, and susceptible therefore to positive definition.

Definitions must, it goes without saying, be definitive, which is to say, fixed. How can they, or the values they represent, be compatible with a relative, fluid universe?

Most people would answer, "They can't. It stands to reason."

And that, precisely, is our difficulty. For our Western heritage dictates also our bias: the belief that reason is the only right way to understand reality, and that things must be either rational (hence, meaningful) or irrational (hence, meaningless).

The German philosopher Hegel put it in these words: "All that is real is rational, and all that is rational is real."

Every civilization has its own special bias. The Japanese like to see life in terms of esthetic perfection. The Chinese once considered heaven an orderly extension of their own refined, orderly culture. The Romans saw the universe as virtually ruled by Roman Law. And

Western civilization, partial heir to the Roman, has always viewed reality in terms of what it has been pleased to call the "light" of reason. Reason, for more than two thousand years, has been not only the cornerstone of our philosophy: It has been the entire edifice.

Our categorical approach has had several very obvious advantages. Lately, however, it is becoming evident that there are also, inherent in this approach, several glaring defects, chief among which is that of assuming that definitions can serve *absolutely* in place of the things they define.

According to the rules of logic, if A is once properly defined as B, it cannot also be not-B; nor can it hover vaguely between B and not-B. It must be definitely what it has been agreed upon to call it. Its opposite, by contrast, must definitely be not-B; it cannot slip over occasionally, perhaps when one is looking the other way, and become B.

See now what has followed from this line of thinking. Because nature does not appear to be meaningful in the way we have always assumed, it must therefore be the opposite of what we've assumed: In other words, it must be meaningless. It isn't B; it must therefore be not-B. Because things do not appear to be rooted in reason, they must therefore be reasonless. Because evolution does not appear to be guided by some rational plan, it must therefore be unplanned, and its multifarious changes all quite purposeless and accidental. Because moral values are not absolute, they must therefore be susceptible to infinite manipulation on the part of human beings.

"Either/or": These words aptly describe the framework within which our entire civilization has evolved.

There is a certain irony in the fact that *reason* has been used to determine that all things are reasonless. Our thinkers have tried so very *sensibly* to demonstrate that nothing makes any sense! Reason's decision that reason doesn't exist rather resembles a fish swimming about in a pool in search of other fish, until at last, finding none, it concludes, "There are no fish in this pool; probably there isn't enough water here for fish to swim in." (Sometimes the scientific objectivity with which we exclude the observer from his observations borders on the lunatic!)

Something seems to be very wrong in our fish pond. It is time for us to examine reason itself and see the extent to which it has prejudiced, instead of clarifying, our approach to reality. How did our methods of reasoning evolve?

The rationalistic approach was first set forth by the ancient Greeks. It was their particular brand of logic, even more so than that of the Romans, which formed virtually the basis of Western civilization.

Aristotle reduced those principles to these simple rules:

1) The Law of *Identity:* A is always the same as A.

2) The Law of *Contradiction:* A cannot be both B and not-B.

3) The Law of *the Excluded Middle:* A must be *either* B *or* not-B.

This system forms, in every field, the cornerstone of traditional Western thought. It directed the investigations of modern science until the turn of the Twentieth Century, and even today provides the guidelines for most scientific investigation.

The merits of the system are obvious. If a scientist had no way of defining his material, and of limiting his work with it to those definitions, he would find it impossible to reach definitive conclusions. If a mathematician were to write that A equals B, and then turn around half-way through his theorem and state that maybe, on the other hand, A doesn't equal B on the first Sunday of each month, he would find it difficult to get a serious hearing.

Alice in Wonderland encountered such difficulties while playing a game of croquet. Her "mallet" turned out to be a flamingo, which kept craning its neck upward to look at her. Her "ball" turned out to be a hedgehog, which persisted in uncurling itself and walking away unconcernedly. Lewis Carroll, the author (Carroll was the *nom de plume* for Charles Dodgson, a famous mathematician), was describing the predicament in which rational thinkers would find themselves, were A to decide not to be A sometimes, just for a pleasant change; or were A, like the hedgehog, to manage to be both B and not-B at the same time; or were A neither specifically B nor very definitely anything else. Whenever a scientist encounters such contradictions, he does his level best to resolve them. Inconsistency is anathema to all systematic logic.

Even in science, however, the firm principles of logic have been most useful in the investigation of purely mechanistic phenomena. As the mathematician and philosopher, J.W.N. Sullivan, put it: "The scientific account of our universe appears clearest and most convincing when it deals with inanimate matter."* As phenomena increase in complexity or in subtlety, it becomes increasingly difficult to confine them to consistent patterns of behavior. In mathematics, if A equals B, and B equals C, then A equals C. Always. In life, however, mathematical principles notwithstanding, A may not equal C nearly so closely as it does B.

No two thumbprints are exactly alike. Living creatures are simply not reducible to perfect equations. *In life, no absolute equals exist.*

Consider this example: X football team may equal Y football team, in the sense that both teams are more or less evenly matched. Y football team, similarly, may equal Z football team. But Z team may invariably trounce X team, in smug defiance of every principle of Grecian logic.

From the physical sciences, with their solid and clearly defined concepts of such things as mass, weight, and motion, it is a long step to such insubstantial questions as those involving living situations and thinking, feeling human beings. It is nevertheless a phenomenon of Western civilization that men have tried to squeeze life as well, with all its countless variations, into the same narrow boxes of categorical reason as those which were built to define material phenomena. They have overlooked this simple truth: *To define is to confine.*

Here is how formal reasoning works when it is

---

* J.W.N. Sullivan, *The Limitations of Science* (Mentor Books, New York, 1959), paperback, p. 125.

applied to life, as opposed to its application to the more clear-cut fields of the physical sciences.

Essentially, in order to reason in the true Aristotelian manner, it is necessary to translate things into conceptual terms. Algebra does this, in a limited sense, by forming its equations with letters instead of with the objects for which those letters stand. But algebra deals with comparatively simple phenomena: weights, measures, motion, and the like. There is a limit to how deeply you can probe, when your material is described by such rudimentary symbols as A, B, and C. The conceptual terms of philosophy, by contrast, concerned as they are with subjects of far greater complexity, must necessarily be couched in more complex terms.

Consider a famous conceptual definition: "Man is a rational animal." St. Thomas Aquinas conceived this one in the classical tradition of Aristotelian logic. To appreciate its very real value, consider these points:

If you were to write about mankind philosophically, to what conceptual post would you tie your dissertation? Would you write about John Burns next door? or about short men and tall men? or young men and old men? It would take you forever to reach universal principles—necessary in any general discussion—at that rate. No, for the purposes of philosophy you would need to abstract from all human phenomena those factors which all men have in common.

Again, you would need to define man in essential terms. The fact that men have eyes would be irrelevant to your purpose, unless vision was the subject of your dissertation.

You would need to look for causes rather than for effects. Men's power of speech, considered even generally, would be a secondary consideration to their ability to think, since the important thing, in most contexts, would be their power to speak *intelligently*.

And, you would want to keep your definition as simple as possible; it would hopelessly overburden your dissertation if your very first principles were already labyrinthine.

You would want to be incisive, but at the same time you'd want your definition to suggest further possibilities of thought; the dictionary definition of man as "a human being" would be a waste to you, for it would take you no farther than the definition itself.

With all these considerations in mind, there is hardly a better definition of man possible than Aquinas's. His simple statement, "Man is a rational animal," is hailed by scholars even today as a masterpiece of philosophical lexicography.

Once the vague term, *man,* is conceptualized by the specific expression, "rational animal," it becomes possible to think about man intelligently in numerous abstract associations: man as a moral being; man as a spiritual being; man in relation to other creatures; man in relation to his Creator. St. Thomas's pithy definition yields an abundance of philosophical opportunities.

Excellent though it is, however, it suffers from the weakness with which all categorical abstractions are afflicted: It is fruitful in the specific sphere of thought for which it was intended, but misleading when applied in any other sphere.

Categorical abstractions represent a deliberate effort to define things *absolutely*. They recognize no other level of abstraction. So it is that, in actual usage, one frequently finds them being *mis*applied. While undeniably an aid to intellectual unfoldment, they can also serve as obstacles to further development.

Human nature being what it is, a constantly growing thing, man's understanding necessarily changes and deepens with time. If, as he grows intellectually, he continues to apply basic concepts in the sense that he first understood them, the very ideas that once clarified his understanding may subsequently prevent him from attaining deeper understanding.

To define is to confine. Conceptual logic limits the expansion of awareness. It presents definitions as fixed and unchangeable, and insists that they be forever the window through which every new experience in life is viewed. What one ought to do, of course, is constantly review his initial concepts in terms of his new life-experiences. Conceptual thinking, however, discourages any such simple exercise of common sense. It is definition-oriented, not experience-oriented. Thus, the rationalist has a marked inclination to come at reality secondhand, as though through a dictionary.

The difficulty, however, is not only long-range, in terms of obstructing the continued growth of understanding: It is also immediate. By defining man as a "rational animal," and limiting our thinking of him to these terms, we may find the definition, in certain contexts, actually distorting the reality.

Is it frivolous to ask of what earthly use it would be to

speak of man as a "rational animal" when referring to his irrational moods? If a definition really is absolute, it should serve us absolutely. But in this case we see that the definition is worse than useless: It is a definite handicap.

Again, what of love? Can this universal feeling be boxed into Aquinas's neat intellectual category? We might somehow reshape our natural understanding of love to view it as either rational or animalistic, or both, but in the process would we not be doing love a great injustice? And while rationalists may imagine that the heart's feelings can be understood perfectly by dry logic alone (their categorical absolutism would tempt them to such an unrealistic belief), anyone who has actually loved knows very well that only by loving can those feelings be even remotely understood.

A categorical concept is a "frozen" image of reality; it can never stand completely in place of the reality it describes, for the simple reason that it is not that reality. The term, "rational animal," is not *identical* with man, though it describes him effectively enough for certain purposes. It leaves out of reckoning innumerable human attributes. Every time, moreover, that the term is given a special application, without fresh reference to the reality that it represents, the definition of that reality becomes diminished further still. Specialized applications of the term, "rational animal," convey still less than the original definition the fullness of what man is.

Applied in relation to other animals, the word "rational" may become more emphasized than its corollary, "animal." ("Oh, yes," one will admit, "it's true that we, too, are animals, but how very different from all the others! Only man is *rational.*") When comparing this "rational animal" to the angels, however, stress may have to be placed on the word, "animal," to provide a necessary contrast between man and the heavenly host. The same term, "rational animal," though used in both cases, would in each case be given a very different slant. In effect, we would not in either case be using the original concept, *but rather a concept of that concept*—an image of the original image of reality.

As the primary concept is not the reality that it represents, so also the secondary concept is only an abstraction, and hence a dilution, of the first one.

Formal reasoning is like tuning a piano. If one tunes the D note to the C note, the E note to the D note, and so on up the scale, relating each note only to the one directly before it, one is almost certain to find after progressing some distance that the highest note is incorrectly tuned to the first. Undetectable variations will have increased by minute degrees, until the difference ends in an outright dissonance. To avoid this progressive error, a piano tuner refers back repeatedly to his basic set of notes.

The deductions of logic, similarly, need to be tested repeatedly against their first principles, and verified wherever necessary by fresh experiments. If a series of deductions is permitted to proceed unchecked, it should be recognized for what it is: a string of conjectures, merely; guesses that may in fact be very far from the facts.

Unfortunately, the temptation of logic is to consider the neatness of its own syllogisms to be proof sufficient that they are accurate.

We have seen how important rationalism was in the development of modern science. Mathematics, physics, and chemistry—unlike philosophy and religion—dealt deliberately with subjects in which the variables were few. Even these few, it was hoped, would eventually be eliminated.

If any field of study should inspire utter confidence in categorical reasoning, it is that of the physical sciences. Yet scientists, far more so than the philosophers and theologians, have learned to beware the witchcraft of reason. By confining their reasoning to questions that would most convincingly prove, if any would, the validity of reason, they have given rationalism a chance also to demonstrate its *dis*advantages. And this it has done with a vengeance.

Basically, rationalism has been found to err in the assumption that if a concept follows logically from a series of known truths, it, too, must be true. Science, in testing such "necessary" lines of logic, has found many a perfectly logical conclusion to be perfectly false.

An excellent case in point is the famous Michelson-Morley experiment in 1887, which conclusively demonstrated a logical "impossibility": that the velocity of light is always the same regardless of the relative speed of its point of origin. On the basis of this discovery, Einstein, with his revolutionary theory of relativity, dealt a deathblow to classical physics.

Experimentation, however, has never been popular with philosophers and religionists.

Immanuel Kant wrote a textbook on pedagogy.

Though a teacher himself, he cheerfully admitted that he had never actually tested any of his own principles.

Arthur Schopenhauer wrote scathingly against women. And what was his experience with the fair sex? Nil, virtually—apart from his own unfortunate relationship with his mother, by whom he felt rejected. Schopenhauer never married; he seems never even to have had a friend of the opposite sex.

Jean Jacques Rousseau based his entire doctrine of the natural goodness of unsophisticated man on his concept of "the noble savage"—a theoretical creature if ever there was one, and one whose reality Rousseau might easily have tested, since even in his day the West had developed a certain amount of contact with primitive peoples.

Søren Kierkegaard taught that a man ought to stand firmly on his own feet as an individual, regally indifferent to the adverse opinion of others. Yet after he himself was criticized in the local scandal sheet, *The Corsair,* he spent years lamenting its ridicule as a "crucifixion."

William James, to prepare himself for writing his famous book, *The Varieties of Religious Experience,* did not consider it necessary to seek out a single living person of spiritual experience, by whose example he might have tested—and incidentally, been obliged to reject—some of his basic ideas. Still less did he try to gain any actual religious experience for himself.

Friedrich Nietzsche, incapacitated for combat duty during the Franco-Prussian War of 1870, served in the army briefly as a nurse. The sight of blood, however, made him physically ill and he had to be sent home. There, in the tranquillity of the Swiss Alps, he developed a philosophy of power to which the almost inevitable corollary was physical violence—indeed, warfare.

And we have already seen the lack of realism in the writings of Jean-Paul Sartre. It would be only fair to add in his excuse that he was at least the heir to an honored tradition.

The more a line of reasoning gets away from tested realities, the greater the danger of its approaching pure fiction.

Strange to say, too, the fewer the chances there are of testing a particular line of reasoning, the more the rationalist tends to dogmatize his conclusions! As we pointed out, axiomatically, in Chapter Two, the dogmatic tendency increases in direct proportion to one's inability to prove a point. The mere willingness to experiment seems to place an automatic curb on man's dogmatic enthusiasms.

Interesting, indeed, is the way that scientific experimentation has undermined the dependence of scientists on reason. As the physical sciences have grown in scope and subtlety, the limitations of their use of categorical logic have become increasingly apparent. Scientific maturity has revealed that many of the seemingly absolute laws on which men so long relied were convenient pegs, merely, on which to hang their ideas.

Newton's laws of motion are now recognized as absolute only if we posit that our universe is a giant mechanism, which it has been proved that it is not.

Euclid's geometry is useful only as long as we think of reality as consisting of straight lines, which we know that it does not. It is easier to work with imaginary straight lines, as long as our working area is small: To apply spherical geometry to the construction of a bookcase would be to introduce unnecessary complications into an otherwise simple undertaking.

And this, in fact—as thinking men are beginning to realize—is what science has always tried to do. Writers of the eighteenth century believed that nature itself is essentially simple, and that it is man who complicates it by the intricacy of his own thought-processes. Today, we know that the shoe fits on the other foot: Whatever the ultimate state of things, the phenomenal universe is *not* simple; it is man who feels a need to simplify his understanding of it in order to be able to work with it at all.

Every scientific law is simply an effort to economize facts; it is not, as was once believed, an absolute definition of reality.

J.W.N. Sullivan expressed this sobering realization in the following words:

> The properties of a triangle, according to Descartes, in no way depend on the human mind. But the invention of the non-Euclidean geometries has taught us that these properties are necessary merely in the sense of being logical consequences of the axioms and postulates with which we start. And these axioms and postulates are arbitrary. They are not necessities of thought; they are matters of the mathematician's caprice. . . . There is no reason to suppose that Descartes's triangle is a revelation of an eternally pre-existing truth—such as a thought in the mind of God. It is an arbitrary creation of the mathematician's

mind, and did not exist until the mathematician thought of it.*

The modern scientist has all but abandoned hope of finding *any* absolutes through his sciences. What he frankly looks for now is the most *convenient* explanation for whatever phenomena he is considering. He is more interested in simplification than in finding ultimate verities. He accepts relativity as perhaps the *only* universal phenomenon. His conscious endeavor is, like an artist, to *frame* various scenes of physical nature; or, like a photographer, to crop his picture of reality in order that his finished view may contain only that which suits his instinctive demand for an order and a symmetry that he can comprehend.

But if reason has been dethroned as the god of the physical sciences, on the solid ground of which it has had its best chance of actually proving itself, how much less may we expect it to give us final and dependable answers on the subject of human life!

We have described logical categories as frozen concepts. What do we mean by a frozen concept? It is a sort of still photograph by which one tries to capture movement in a motionless pose.

Conceptual logic resembles what the ancient Greek philosopher Zeno pulled out of his hat when he declared, "An arrow at any given moment of its flight must be at rest at some particular point." He offered this argument as a proof that the arrow never really

---

* Ibid., p. 152. We shall consider in a later chapter whether Sullivan, in pointing out the relativity of scientific "truths," has not gone too far in calling them, therefore, "matters of . . . caprice."

moves at all! But perhaps, to be fair, all he really wanted to do was demonstrate the inadequacy of logic itself.

It is the eternal dream of the rationalist to gather, by means of his frozen definitions, enough information on any given subject ultimately to know everything there is to know about it, and thereby to master it absolutely. A pipe dream, truly! Reason alone, especially where questions of conscious, ever-fluctuating life are concerned, cannot ever, not remotely possibly, supply the key to total mastery that it promises.

Supposing one were taught to pick up a fork by first memorizing the countless muscles involved in the maneuver; their unique, separate functions, and their several purposes in a synchronized action; the exact stress needed in each muscle to offset that exerted by all the other muscles brought into play; the weight of the fork; the exact part of the fork that one must grasp to ensure the accuracy of his assembled data on muscular stress; the possibility of slippage on the fork due to excessive moisture in the fingers; the danger of someone's making a particularly obnoxious remark about the whole procedure just when the fork is at last on the point of being inserted into the mouth, a vigorous reply becoming thereby suddenly necessary. To gather *all* the pertinent information would take forever; it is doubtful, indeed, whether it could ever be assembled completely. But even if it were, of what practical use would it be? Too many details of this simple operation would only complicate it hopelessly.

A billion stationary points along the arrow's course still would not explain the simple fact of its movement.

A music teacher in my high school claimed to have discovered a revolutionary technique for teaching students how to sing. The voice, he pointed out, is produced by a series of individual staccato croaks. He reasoned that if one will only concentrate on producing those separate croaks, and then slowly join them together with increasing rapidity, the final result will be—hold your breath—yes, a VOICE!

All the students of his method were still, last heard from, in the frog stage. But there, anyway, was a most philosophical teacher, a tried and true Aristotelian! He didn't succeed in improving anyone's voice, but he did succeed in neatly breaking down a simple, familiar function into some of its numerous unfamiliar parts. The vocal introspection that he recommended was meant to give his students perfect understanding of the way their voices worked, and to help them thereby to produce perfect vocal tones. In fact, however, all that his method ever accomplished was distract their attention from the natural flow of singing, and thereby interfere with their normal vocal functioning.

Go out some time onto the playgrounds of your nearest school, and observe there the children at play. Who among them make the best athletes? Those, invariably, who are the most relaxed and natural in their movements. The ones who make the worst athletes, by contrast, are those who seem not to be concentrated on their movements as such, but on the static positions of their arms and legs, as if they were pondering what to do with them.

Even when an expert athlete concentrates carefully

on the positions of his arms and legs in order to master some new technique, his effort is directed toward assimilating those positions as soon as possible into his overall sense of movement. Only after such assimilation can he function again at top efficiency.

Reason often provides a helpful guide to action, but it can never be successfully made the supreme or only guide.

An amusing example of the debilitating effect of too much reasoning is related from the life of Immanuel Kant. Kant insisted that a person's actions should always be guided by the calm deliberations of reason. Will Durant tells us in his book, *The Story of Philosophy:* "Twice he thought of offering his hand to a lady; but he reflected so long that in one case the lady married a bolder man, and in the other the lady removed from Königsberg before the philosopher could make up his mind." Kant never did marry.

The farther one gets away from pure science, the less the principles of pure logic apply. In this respect, indeed, the only "pure" science is mathematics, which deals purely with theory.

But in that case, and with even science's increasing skepticism of reason as the final arbiter, what future is there for reason as the determiner of moral and spiritual values? Must reason be abandoned altogether? This would be, certainly, a very Aristotelian reaction: either we accept reason, or we reject it completely! In fact, this very alternative underscores reason's incapacity to provide us with the answer. How, indeed, could it be reasonably expected, by following its own methodology, to find better alternatives to itself?

The fact is, Reason—that *"belle dame sans merci"*—hath us in thrall, and even when we try to break out of our rational enclosure, we only move in such a way that the trap pinches in another place.

We see an example of this predicament in the earnest effort that was made to escape the imperatives of logic by Alfred Korzybski, founder of the school of General Semantics. Korzybski pointed out many of the disadvantages of Aristotelian logic. The cure he prescribed, however, was, if anything, worse than the disease.

He pointed out, as we have done, that word-definitions are not identical to the objects they describe. How then, he asked, is a person ever to say clearly what he means? One may speak of his neighbor Jim, but to which Jim is he referring? To Jim as he is nowadays? or to Jim as he was ten or twenty years ago? For Jim at different stages of his life has been, in many respects, very different persons. How then are we to speak of him meaningfully?

Korzybski claimed that it is really very simple. All that one needs to do is write Jim's name thus: Jim_{1960} or Jim_{1980} to indicate to which aspect of Jim's life one is referring.

Well, that seems simple enough. But—hmmm, on second thought, here's something else to consider: Jim may be different in the morning from in the evening. Maybe, again, a distinction should be drawn between Jim in the morning *before* breakfast, and Jim *after* breakfast. And what about the weather? Cloudy days may affect him one way; sunny days, another. Is it Jim on a weekend in June we are describing, and not Jim on a November weekday at the office? And if so, was his

CRYSTAL

CLARITY

Dear Dick:

Don asked me to send you
a copy of this, his latest book.

I hope you enjoy it!

Please let me know if there is
anything else I can do for
you. My phone number is 530-
478-7606. E-mail is
seanm@crystalclarity.com.

Warm Regards,

Sean Meshorer

wife in a good humor that day? Were his children well-behaved? Sometimes, come to think of it, Jim may be more like his old 1960 self nowadays than he was, frequently, back when he *was* his old 1960 self.

I can just imagine the endless series of qualifications after Jim's name that a general semanticist would feel himself obliged to use if he were really conscientious about following Korzybski's principles. Far better, I should think, to take a vow of perpetual silence!

The point is, we find here an approach that tries seriously to discover a logical way out of the Aristotelian corral, and all that it does, while working to ease the pressure on one side of the trap, is increase it on the other side.

The fault lies with the fact that every system of thought creates its own conceptual enclosure. The concepts formed within a particular system can reach to the periphery of that system, but cannot penetrate beyond it, *simply because they are a part of the system itself.* As Sullivan put it, discussing this dilemma as it relates to modern physics: "Why is it that the elements of reality [physics] ignores never come in to disturb it? *The reason is that all the terms of physics are defined in terms of one another.*" (Italics ours.)

What, then, is the way out? Romanticists would say, "It's very easy. Simply ignore reason, and get in touch with your feelings." The present need, however, is not to ignore reason, but to learn to use it in new ways, so as not to be limited by the "either/or" approach to reality that is our Grecian heritage. Feeling, moreover, needs to be balanced by reason. When it is not, it loses the capacity to be intuitive, and becomes mere emotionalism, clouding every issue and clarifying nothing.

There is another possible way out of logic's enclosure: We can seek out some *new* system of thought—one, especially, that might be adaptable to the special philosophical needs of our times, which is to say, to the new world-view of modern science.

Historically, revolutions in thinking have often, and perhaps always, occurred as a consequence of exposure to other systems of thought. This happened, for example, in the West with the revolution of modern science.

Medieval rationalism had been a perfect system unto itself. There was no way out of it—not, at any rate, so long as the system itself was adhered to. The Church was authorized to interpret divine revelation. And by whom was it authorized? By Jesus Christ in the Bible, when he said to Peter, "Thou art Peter, and on this rock I will build my church; and the gates of hell shall not prevail against it." (Matthew 16:18) And how was one to know for certain that by these words Jesus meant to confer such authorization on the Church? (After all, he often used similarly concrete words symbolically.) Because the Church said this was what he meant. And how did the Church know? Because theirs was the task of interpreting divine revelation.

It was a perfect argument in a circle. The only avenue by which the human spirit could escape to new vistas lay outside this ideational enclosure. And this was the path science found, through its unprecedented method of testing its hypotheses by experimentation.

Science too, however, was still caught in the greater

web of Greek rationalism. Our very discovery of the limitations of reason has only shown us the *need* to break out of the system. It has not in itself led us outside the system.

Much has been written, particularly since the time of John Stuart Mill, on the supposedly un-Aristotelian method of scientific reasoning. Aristotle, we are told, reasoned *deductively:* From general principles he deduced specific conclusions. Science, by contrast, is said to reason *in*ductively: From specific facts it draws general principles. The difference, however, is not so great as is claimed.

Scientific reasoning is not actually opposed to Aristotelian logic. It is only the other side of the same coin. Both methods of reasoning are simply means of reducing natural phenomena to rational categories. Both represent an attempt to set reality in a firm mold of definitions.

The dividing line between the two systems is, moreover, anything but sharp and clear. For it is doubtful whether general principles are ever conceived *a priori,* without at least some prior reference to specific facts. It is not possible to think in an ideational vacuum. Nor would facts by themselves seem meaningful enough to merit scientific interest, had scientists not already some preexisting hypothesis to which to relate them.

Nor has science been able to kill the spirit of dogmatism that is so inherent in our rationalistic heritage.

Alexis Carrel, in *Man, the Unknown,* wrote that scientists, like people in other fields, have a "natural tendency to reject the things that do not fit into the frame of the scientific or philosophic beliefs of our time. . . . They willingly believe that facts that cannot be explained by current theories do not exist."

And Max Planck, the famous German physicist, wrote in his *Scientific Autobiography:* "A new scientific truth does not triumph by convincing its opponents and making them see the light, but rather because its opponents eventually die, and a new generation grows up that is familiar with it."

A revolution in our thinking is the need of the hour. If ideational revolutions require going outside the current systems, then let us see what other systems are available. In them, we may at least find a hint of new directions for ourselves.

In medieval times, the answer came from outside the Church. Today, perhaps it will come from outside our own civilization, the entire structure of which is framed in rationalism.

One advantage to living in the modern age is the contact that easy transport and communication have given us with peoples all over the world. Somewhere, in all this diversity, there may exist systems of thought that are different from our own, yet sufficiently like our own to be compatible with it. For what we want, essentially, is not to abandon that which is good in our own system, but only to infuse our system with new insights. This is what happened, for example, with the reawakened interest in Greek civilization that brought about the Renaissance in Italy.

What we need today, in other words, is a *New* Renaissance.

Paramhansa Yogananda, the great Indian sage, won a Western critic to his side when he said to him: "We are all of us a little bit crazy, but most of us don't know it because we mix only with people with the same type of craziness as our own. See, then, what an opportunity you and I have to learn from each other. It is only when differently crazy people come together that they get a chance to find out the errors in their own types of craziness!"

Witty words, and wise! If only we can find some civilization with an approach to reality that accepts relativism without being shaken by it, we may have discovered a philosophical gold mine. For any civilization that can embrace relativism and live may well have found exactly the cure we need for our own present disease.

In the next three chapters we shall consider the possible contributions of one civilization which, I am convinced, has just the right antidote for us. Its approach to life is the counterpart, on a human, philosophical, and spiritual level, to the revolution in thinking that has been going on in the physical sciences.

Meanwhile, let us reflect whether our discovery that reason is, after all, only a wooden idol is not cause for rejoicing rather than for despair.

Take a glance at the furrowed brows, the burdened gaze, the ironic smile of people who wander all their lives in a desert of dry logic. They are thinking *about* life; they are not *living*. Is that our image of the ideal man? Is it what we ourselves wish to be like?

How many popular heroes of modern novel, stage, and television try to demonstrate their superiority to the rest of us social pygmies by never laughing, never grieving over the sorrows of others, never meeting others sympathetically on their own level, nor ever rejoicing at the wonder and beauty of life.

"Keep your eyes on the road," says our logical super-man curtly, when his cab driver ventures some harmless pleasantry. "You poor, foolish mortal!" his lofty sneer seems to imply, when a woman or a child marvels at the riot of color in a sunset. Our logical hero, too, is a wooden idol. His halo of superiority is formed of an absence, and not of any fullness, of life.

But what does it mean, when one's wooden idols are destroyed? Need one's faith be destroyed with them?

Leo Tolstoy wrote: "When a savage ceases to believe in his wooden god, this does not mean that there is no God, but only that the true God is not made of wood."

CHAPTER SIX

Catching the Right Wave

The categorical logic of Western thought has shown itself incapable of finding purpose and meaning in a universe revealed as fluid, not fixed.

In this chapter we seek a philosophy that is attuned to the findings of modern science, and discover a view of life which, though explicitly relativistic, gives promise of providing a profound and workable system of values.

CHAPTER SIX

Catching the Right Wave

DIFFERENCES OF OUTLOOK the world over have been, for me personally, a lifelong fascination.

I was given a good push in this direction by the fact of being born outside my own country. Both my parents were American, but my father worked for fifteen years as a geologist in Rumania. My home was that country until the age of thirteen, during which time I was also sent to school in Switzerland and in England. This was the period before World War II, when no iron curtain divided Eastern from Western Europe. My parents' friends belonged to many different nationalities.

Thus, I grew up in an international setting, in which I found the variety of national characteristics endlessly fascinating. The very multiplicity of accents, which my brothers and I often played at imitating, awakened in us an awareness of people not only as individuals, but also as Americans, British, Austrians, Rumanians.

Looking back, I still recall with fascination some of the characteristics that came into focus for me: the solid common sense of the English; the practicality of the Scots; the affectation of importance in the way so many Americans spoke, but the friendly sense of humor of many others; the blustering, somewhat fanciful idealism of the Irish; the intellectual independence, but also the charm, of the French; the self-assurance of the Austrians; the "thing"-centeredness of the Swiss; the people-centeredness of the Italians; the snowplow efficiency of the Germans; the cheerful inefficiency of the Rumanians.

There was another side to all this diversity. These people were our friends. It was obvious to us children that the variety they displayed was superficial, like the differences one finds in any family. We called our parents' friends "Uncle" and "Auntie," and looked on them as our own. Thus, we were conditioned also from the beginning to a sense of the underlying similarity of people everywhere.

When we moved back to America with the outbreak of World War II, I faced a painful process of adjustment, for I found myself not nearly so American as I had always proudly imagined. This traumatic period in my life helped also, however, to keep alive in me the sense of kinship with the people of all nations, while it weakened whatever pride I'd had in the mere fact of being American.

Since my childhood I have traveled extensively, and visited more than fifty countries. And I have continued to enjoy observing the superficial differences of national outlook and temperament, while at the same time viewing those differences with empathy, and recognizing underneath them a shared humanity.

In Japan, I was struck by the Japanese dedication to

capturing perfection in everything they do, as if trying to freeze reality in the still pose of a perfect ideal. In Bali, I found the people smilingly indifferent to the concept of *capturing* perfection, which they sought only to reflect, rather, in fluid motion. In Thailand, I encountered a happy confidence in the Thai people that everything would always work out for the best. In Cambodia, in 1958, I sensed a somber cloud over the consciousness of the country. In Fiji, I was charmed by the "today-is-all-that-matters" insouciance of the islanders. And in Arab lands, I was struck by the game many play of concealing their true intentions from others.

It was in India that I met my greatest challenges. I lived in that country for four years.

India's is the oldest civilization in the world. Despite its enormous antiquity, however, the way the ancient Sanskrit texts describe the universe around us seems amazingly contemporary.

The ancient texts tell of a universe billions of years old, and at the same time infinitely vast. They speak of our earth as only one among countless millions of planets. They measure the history of mankind in the millions of years.

How different, their view, from the narrow vistas of time and space that were accepted in the West until only decades ago!

The discovery in our times that light is both a particle and a wave is bewildering to the Western mind. Reason tells us that light ought to be clearly either one thing or the other. For the Indian, however, no such bewilderment exists. He accepts the fact that contradictions inhere in the universe, the very foundation of which is the law of opposition, or duality.* Such is his conditioning, indeed, that he is enamored of paradoxes.

Science has proved that all physical objects, in appearance so infinitely diverse, are in fact only varied manifestations of formless energy. A new thought? Long ago, the *rishi*s, or sages, of India wrote in their *Veda*s (the source-books of Indian civilization):

"They who see but one in all the changing manifoldness of this universe, unto them belongs eternal Truth—unto none else, unto none else."

Again, the Indian has no difficulty in dealing with a modern discovery that has many Westerners questioning the very nature of consciousness. The Westerner, accustomed as he is to identifying his consciousness with his ability to think, and to deducing his spiritual nature from his capacity to reason, is disturbed by the discovery that the human brain is only a sort of electronic thinking machine. The French philosopher Descartes even offered the phenomenon of thought as his famous "proof" of man's existence: *"Cogito, ergo sum"*: "I think, therefore I am." And the great theologian St. Thomas Aquinas, with his definition of man as a "rational animal," sought to sum up man's spiritual, as distinct from his physical, nature in this single fact of his ability to reason.

---

* *Dwaita* in Sanskrit; the natural oppositions of light and darkness, heat and cold, pleasure and pain, etc. None of these would be conceivable without its opposite. The very existence of light implies the complementary existence of darkness; of heat, that of cold; and so forth. Nor are these "pairs of opposites" only conceptual. Positive and negative polarity is inherent to the structure of the atom. The principle of duality is fundamental to the Indian concept of relativity.

It is a blow indeed to such an appraisal of mankind to discover that when a person reasons he is simply "manipulating memory traces" in the brain—a job that machines can be programmed to do as well, or even better!

To the Indian, however, this discovery of the mechanical aspects of thinking is merely fascinating; it is not morally or spiritually shattering. He has always considered the brain to be but a tool for his higher Self to use, much as the brain itself uses the eyes and the muscles of the body. Armed with this concept, the Indian finds it natural to point out that, after all, no "thinking machine" can run itself; it needs an operator. Similarly, the brain needs the "operator" of the higher Self, which works through the brain rather than as an aspect of the brain's own functioning.

Finally, as regards changing the human personality with a surgeon's knife—"Well," the Indian asks, "what does this prove, since the personality is not the Self anyway?"

To continue to the question of religion, the informed Indian attitude is not sectarian. India hasn't even a name for its own indigenous religion. Many centuries ago, foreign invaders gave to the religion they found in that country the name, "Hinduism." Indians themselves, however, have always called their religion, *Sanatan Dharma*, "The Eternal Religion"—a term which, properly understood, embraces equally all the religions of the world. *Sanatan Dharma* has never been considered exclusively the property of India's religion and culture.

In the broad-mindedness of this attitude we find similarities, again, to the open-mindedness of modern science.

Especially apposite to the subject of this book is another basic attitude that I encountered during my years in India: an acceptance of experience over reason as the final arbiter in the search for truth. This practical attitude anticipates, on a level of human values, the methodology of modern science with its constant emphasis on experimentation.

In India's expansive view of reality, and in her insistence on direct experience over logical syllogisms, she appears to have been at home for many centuries on plateaus of thought to which only a few advance scouts from the West have climbed, and that only in this century.

So far, the challenge of Indian thought is an exciting voyage of discovery. Somewhere about now in that voyage, however, the Western student of Indian thought suddenly runs into what looks to him like a stone wall of illogic. I myself became aware of the problem as it dawned on me, gradually, how much at sea many Indians were with Western logic. With astonishing frequency I would hear someone declare confidently, "This *proves* that . . ." when it did nothing of the kind, and at best merely suggested a possibility.*

In the West, raised as we are in the long shadow of Aristotelian logic, the rational principles of "either/or" have for millennia been so basic to our way of thinking that we take them completely for granted as simple necessities of thought. To us, then, ultimate agreement in any discussion

---

* Westerners love the story, though I'm sure it's apocryphal, of the Hindu guide who announced proudly to an American visitor, "In all the excavations they have done in our country, they have never discovered so much as a single wire. This *proves* that in ancient India they had the wireless!"

is almost a point of honor: "Either we agree to this idea, or we agree to reject it. There can be no in betweens."

In India I discovered (at first, to my dismay) that for Indians the universe need not be reasonable at all—not, at least, in the Aristotelian sense—for it to be deeply meaningful. The Indians I met—highly intelligent, well educated men and women—seemed perfectly contented to differ with me in any discussion without at the same time calling my position wrong. I found them baffled, moreover, by my insistence that some sort of agreement had always to be reached, as if absolutes were at stake.

The Western pursuit of reality might be likened to a tennis match: truth forever on one side, falsehood on the other, and between the two a dividing net, forever fixed and immovable. Western relativists might insist that the two sides be interchangeable. And Sartre might even ask rhetorically, "Who needs a net?" Indians, on the other hand, would say, "No, leave the net in place. Just keep it movable."

To the Indian, truth and falsehood have no absolute demarcations. They maintain their relative positions to each other. It is just that the net is movable toward either side, such that most of True's side of the court may, on occasion, be apportioned to False, or most of False's side, to True. Individual circumstances will determine the placing of the net. Depending on where, relative to the net's position, a particular statement of belief lies, it may be either true or false.

I was not alone in my perplexity before this alien view of things.

I remember a conversation I had with a missionary

priest in India. In his homeland, Belgium, he had been carefully trained in the syllogisms of Aristotelian logic. In India, he'd been given the highly imaginative assignment of teaching Hindu philosophy at a Jesuit college in the town of Ranchi.

"It's incredible!" he exclaimed heatedly. "These Indians will tell you in all earnestness that they find inspiration in the Bible, that they love Jesus Christ, that they agree completely with everything he said, and with everything *you* say, and yet—they remain Hindus!"

I was often told during my four years in India that few Hindu students at the mission schools and colleges—perhaps even none of them—ever became converted to Christianity.

This Belgian priest was convinced that there was some basic flaw in the character of Indians that prevented them from calling anything absolutely one thing or another. "They just can't seem to make up their minds!" he cried exasperatedly, waving his arms above his head in the very opposite of a Gallic shrug.

Many a Westerner, exposed for any length of time to Hindu civilization, has expressed similar exasperation. To him, the Indian attitude toward truth appears vague, without clear perceptions and principles. Many Western religious writers have accused the Indian teachings of being inconsistent. Indian philosophy, to them, seems unformed by any coherent discipline, and Indian religion, universal to the point of creedlessness.

To the Indian, on the other hand, the Western approach seems naive, unrealistic, and narrowly dogmatic. The Indian admires the West for its achievements in the physical sciences, but he considers the rigidity of the Western view of life—the patterns of which are so obviously more flexible than the axioms of geometry—to be a sign of philosophical immaturity.

Which view is correct? Each, unquestionably, has its own special merits; it is probably not a simple case of "either/or." One notes with interest, however, that it is the Indian view, far more than the Western, that is geared to the fluid realities perceived by modern science.

Relativity forms the basis of a major portion of Indian philosophy. Time, space, the seemingly solid "reality" of matter: None of these is considered absolute.

Despite India's calm acceptance of values as relative, the Indian people as a whole are recognized the world over as being among the most deeply moral of all peoples. A number of them (Mahatma Gandhi was but one example) have inspired millions by the firmness of their moral vigor. One might almost imagine them to have been exponents of Kantian absolutism. And yet, these are a people who accept as a simple matter of fact that moral values are relative!

Indians do not see relativism as diminishing the reality of right and wrong. They merely explain right and wrong differently from the way we've been accustomed to do.

Of particular interest to us in these pages is the fact that, while the Indian outlook is in many ways so well adapted, on a level of human values, to the findings of modern science, it in no way joins Sartre in heralding meaninglessness as the Final Answer. Nor does its acknowledgment of relativity, whether in physics or on a level of values, signify a denial that moral values are real and binding on human behavior. Quite the contrary, their philosophy covers a range of some of the loftiest themes ever conceived by man, broad enough to have inspired some of the greatest thinkers in the West.

Ralph Waldo Emerson wrote, in his *Journal,* of the impact Vedic thought had had on him:

"It is sublime as heat and night and a breathless ocean. It contains every religious sentiment, all the grand ethics which visit in turn each noble poetic mind."

And the German philosopher Schopenhauer wrote, in *Parerga,* of the *Upanishads* (the summations of the *Vedas*):

"It is the most profitable and most elevating reading that is possible in the world."

India's approach to the question of values is of inestimable value to the present-day search for meaning. For it complements Western thought, rather than pursuing completely unrelated lines of inquiry.

The world-wide trend at present is toward cultural synthesis. For hundreds of years in the past, the nations developed in comparative isolation from one another. Each perfected certain virtues and skills. Each in its own way achieved a certain level of greatness. Each culture, however, was also one-sided in its development. Some directed their energy toward the arts; others, toward warfare; still others, toward agriculture or toward developing the social graces. Each would have been more perfectly balanced, and achieved greatness more truly, had it absorbed some of the virtues that were the characteristics of other nations.

Often, indeed, it was by exposure to other cultures that societies in the past received fresh impetus in their own development. One thinks of Florence during the Renaissance, following the rediscovery of the beauty in realism of Greek art; of the Arabs, following their conquests in India; of the Greco-Roman civilization under the impact of Christianity; and, more recently, of the interest in human consciousness over material acquisition that flowered in America after the impact with Japanese culture, following World War II.

Today, with the advances of modern science, and with common access to rapid transport and communication, the nations of the world are being drawn together as if into a single room. It is as though Destiny herself had ordained the mélange, to give peoples everywhere a chance to learn from one another, and, in the exchange, to achieve levels of greatness hitherto not seen on earth.

The waves of many cultures are rolling toward our shores. And we, like surfers, can decide which of these many waves to catch. Some of them will no doubt carry us farther than others. Many countries and many cultures have already shown that they have something to teach us. Among these, the genius of India, particularly, offers insights into human values and consciousness which presently concern the very future of our civilization.

Let us consider seriously the possibility that the answers we need may be awaiting us, not only in a general way outside our own traditions, but more specifically in the insights of ancient India.

Let us look particularly at what we can learn from them about truth in relativity, and see whether they may offer us practical solutions to the present-day problem of meaninglessness.

CHAPTERS SEVEN and EIGHT

Truth in Relativity
Parts I and II

In the Indian view, relativity is a unitive, not a divisive, phenomenon. It implies a relationship and an essential harmony among all things. In this view, the relativity of human values suggests, not a meaningless tangle, but a progressively growing insight and understanding.

The child grows up to become a man; there is a corresponding development in his understanding. Values, here, are relative because the rules that apply to the child no longer apply, or apply in different ways, to the man.

We see, then, that the relativity of values is directional. And this direction is a matter of universal experience. Far from providing man with an excuse for moral irresponsibility, this common-sense view of reality actually holds out hope for continuous evolution, for indefinite progress. And it justifies a profound assumption of personal responsibility.

CHAPTER SEVEN

Truth in Relativity Part I

THE DISCIPLINE OF EXPERIENCE

LOGIC IN ITS HEYDAY, before the scientific method gained ascendancy, was often treated in a way reminiscent of the tailors in Hans Christian Andersen's story, "The Emperor's New Clothes." People used it to sew elaborate garments of theory, without the help of a single thread of facts, and from cloth that had been woven out of thin air.

Since the dawn of science, however, people have begun to insist that they be shown the thread, and be made to feel the cloth. Science has conditioned us to confine our inquiries into reality to answerable questions.

In the beginning, the questions it asked were quite basic. Philosophers and poets, eager to get on to nobler issues, found the investigations of science not only suffocating, but hopelessly pedestrian.*

---

* "There was a rainbow once in heaven," lamented the poet Keats. "Now it is listed in the catalogue of common things."

Even scientists must sometimes have longed for the freedom to soar up into the skies of speculation, leaving far below them the brown fields of mundane facts that they were committed to plowing. Their scientific method may often have pinned the sad wings of fancy, and torn down the enticing web of reason. The harvest of their conscientious labor, however, has been not only plentiful, but exotic, beyond the wildest dreams of poets and philosophers. Scientists, by disciplining themselves to operate within the framework of demonstrable facts, have discovered a freedom never heard of before.

What mere rationalist could have conceived of cosmic space as expanding, and therefore finite? or of space as curved? or of matter as not even solid? Anyone arriving at such conclusions by logic alone would have been dismissed as insane. It is experience that has gradually opened the windows of thought onto such staggering vistas.

Scientists no longer fear to step beyond the pale of reason. Their tests have too often belied reason's ponderous judgments.

Success in one field of thought, however, has introduced bedlam into another. Throughout the present scientific era, man's understanding of moral and spiritual values has been limping painfully behind the material sciences as they stride purposefully toward the horizon.

Adjustment to new discoveries is always a struggle. Scientists have at least had the advantage of a framework that gave them room for their discoveries. No space, unfortunately, exists within that framework for such intangibles as moral values.

Philosophers, theologians, and others of more or less idealistic bent have found no alternate method to that of science with which they might oppose science's more materialistic orientation. Science, for them, in their continued reliance on the supremacy of logic, has proved a disaster. Every new scientific discovery has only left them gazing around helplessly at the shattered remains of yet another set of beliefs. Old definitions of moral and spiritual values lie about their feet in piles of rubble. Old truths have been knocked off their pedestals. And science, meanwhile, the bull in this antique china shop, moves serenely on its way as though nothing could possibly be wrong.

The main effort so far, in the field of philosophy, has been directed at gluing the broken pieces together again. Only a few thinkers like Sartre—the *enfants terribles* of contemporary thought—have exulted in the confusion.

It is the special contribution of India's ancient discoveries that they bridge the gap between philosophy and modern science. For they introduce into moral and spiritual spheres the concept of limiting man's acceptance of non-material truths to those concepts which, like the concepts of science, can be tested and proved.

India's traditional attitude is one of philosophical naturalism—of concern with what *is,* rather than with what might be, or with what we might believe ought to be.

The Indian approach, like that of modern science, is rational without being rationalistic. It is philosophical without sacrificing practicality. And, although pragmatic, it doesn't sacrifice poetic vision. Indeed, many of its most profound utterances were couched in poetic meter and metaphor.

The Indian approach differs from that of modern science in that it is not concerned with mechanisms. For this reason it does not employ mechanical methods in its experiments. It makes no precondition—as science did until only recently—that for a thing to be real one must be able to make a model of it. Its method, on the other hand, is admirably adapted to the realities with which it deals.

Naturalism, in the Indian sense of the word, completely by-passes the Western logicians' battleground of "either/or." It sees no reason why the universe should forever be either one thing or another—either wholly rational, for example, or wholly irrational. It poses no *a priori* conditions on the subjects that it studies. Rather, it asks simply of life, "What are the facts?"

On the basis of this simple question, Indian seekers of truth embarked millennia ago on a voyage of discovery that took them to heights that are comparable to the loftiest speculations of modern science.

And yet, this further point needs to be made: Unlike science, Indian thought, even at those rarefied heights, is *not* speculative.

Herein, however, lies the true similarity between Indian philosophy and modern science: *Both place constant, paramount emphasis on workability.*

Western philosophical, ethical, and religious thought has never shown any such practical concern. As we have already seen, the West's geniuses of philosophical speculation have seldom troubled to test even their most verifiable theories.

Kant never bothered to apply in the classroom his own precepts on pedagogy. Schopenhauer made no first-hand study of women before writing diatribes against them; his experience with the fair sex was considerably less than that of the average man.

It is this facet of Indian culture that strikes one as most particularly significant from a point of view of the modern challenge of meaninglessness: *its constant stress on experience over untested theory.*

Many Westerners, caught in a web of their traditional logic, claim that Indian thought soared too high above the conceptual powers of the human mind to be acceptable. As an answer to their claim, it may help to point out that India's approach to reality has not been devoid of practical results in those spheres which we recognize as specifically the hunting grounds of modern science. For the conclusions India reached long ago were the same as some of the most advanced in modern physics and engineering.

The Indian cosmography, born in antiquity, strikes one today as amazingly modern. Expressions were used, to be sure, that strike us today as quaint, their terminology reminiscent of a bygone age. Explanations, moreover, were often given metaphorically, as one might expect of a culture that was oriented more to man's inner life than to conquering objective Nature. And yet, in the midst of this exotic jungle of alien concepts and vocabulary, the present-day Westerner stumbles frequently on open clearings where, unexpectedly, the terrain looks very familiar.

He learns, for example, as I mentioned in the last

chapter, that India has never limited its conception of time to a few crowded millennia. Thousands of years ago, her sages computed the earth's age at over two billion years, our present era being what they called the seventh *manvantra,* each *manvantra* encompassing many millions of years. This is a staggering claim, considering how much scientific evidence was needed in our time before men could even contemplate so vast a time scale.*

Another modern-sounding, but in fact ancient, teaching concerns the vastness of the physical universe. For this view one must look not to popular mythology, which, like folklore everywhere, is a mixed bag of fantasy and symbolism. Rather, one must look to India's deliberately scientific treatises.

An ancient treatise, the *Laya Yoga Samhita,* stated: "Just as beams of sunlight reveal in a room the presence of innumerable motes, so infinite space is filled with countless solar systems (*brahmandas*)." (Not many centuries ago, Westerners were still theorizing that the stars were lights hanging down from the inverted bowl of the nocturnal sky. To the naked eye, in fact, that is more or less what they may appear to be.)

Serious dissertations described also the infinitesimal smallness of things. The atomic structure of matter— proved by science only in this Twentieth Century—was discussed in the ancient *Vaisesika* treatises. And in another treatise, the *Yoga Vashishta,* it was stated, in a

---

* And the Church has lagged far behind science in this respect. An appendix, dated 1924, in my copy of the Holy Bible solemnly declares that the period from the Creation to the birth of Jesus Christ was only 4003 years.

passage comparable to the foregoing: "There are vast worlds all placed away within the hollows of each atom, multifarious as the motes in a sunbeam."

Whence came these amazingly enlightened insights? The question itself is fascinating. Fascinating, too, has been the discovery of engineering marvels in ancient times: the radiant heating in the homes, for example, and the modern-style sewage system in the ruins of the five-thousand-year-old cities of Mohenjo-Daro and Harappa.

There are accounts in the ancient texts of flying machines (*vamanas*, as they were called), and also descriptions of how those machines were constructed.

There are accounts of weapons that today remind us forcibly, in the devastation they created, of atom bombs.

In mathematics, too, the ancients achieved a high level of sophistication. It is, incidentally, to India, and not (as many believe) to the Arabs, that we are indebted for the concept of the zero, without which higher mathematics would be impossible.

Passing on to comparisons between the modern scientific method and India's ancient system for ascertaining moral and spiritual values, we find here again a striking similarity.

The first question the Indian seers posed to any proposition was not, "Does it make good theoretical sense?" but rather, "Does it work?" The truth of a claim had to be verified by experience. Reason was given only supportive value in the search for understanding.

In justification of this practical outlook, there is a delightful Indian folk tale about a book-learned philosopher who hired a boat to cross the river Ganges.

Part way across the river, this philosopher, vain of his learning, asked the boatman whether that worthy fellow had read the first of the four Hindu *Veda*s.

"I'm sorry, sir," the boatman replied. "I'm too busy earning a living to devote any time to study."

Smugly the philosopher informed him, "In that case, my good man, a quarter of your life is as good as lost."

The boatman swallowed this insult, and continued to ply his oars. They reached the halfway point in their crossing, when the sage inquired haughtily, "Good man, pray tell me, have you read the second of the four *Veda*s?"

"Most honorable philosopher!" cried the boatman exasperatedly, "I've already told you: I never have any time for reading."

"In that case," the other pompously announced, "not a quarter merely, but half your life is as good as lost."

The scholar seemed prepared to continue in this vein until he'd covered all four of the *Veda*s. All of a sudden, however, a mighty storm swept over the water's surface. Ever larger the waves grew, tossing their little boat helplessly about until it began filling with water. The minutes passed desperately. At last, the boatman shouted above the howling wind:

"Most honored philosopher, you've asked me two questions. Now I must ask you one: Can you swim?"

"Not a stroke!" quavered the scholar, as he clung in despair to an oar.

"In that case," cried the boatman, "it grieves me to inform you that the *whole* of your life will very soon be lost!"

So saying, he dived into the water and, with mighty

strokes, swam to the opposite bank. But the philosopher, though he might have defined water, wind, and the saving act of swimming to any lexicographer's satisfaction, was none the better off for his theoretical knowledge. The boat sank, taking him with it, and his learning was never heard of again.

The moral of this story is clear: It is better to be able to swim through the storms of life than to know how to explain them away by theoretical reason.

In Indian philosophy, explanations are given also—plenty of them, in fact. Always, however, the emphasis is on the direct test of experience.

What sorts of tests, one might ask, can philosophy provide that are comparable to the solid proofs of the physical sciences? Science was distinguished at the outset by its concern with fundamentals: mass, weight, and motion. Philosophy, as we understand the word in the West, is entirely speculative—the more abstract its flights of fancy, the more admirable. The very word, "philosophy," comes from two Greek words which, combined, mean, "the love of wisdom." Western philosophy, in other words, rooted as it is in Aristotelian logic, does not even presume to *know* the truth (that is, to be wise), but only claims to *love* truth—or, more accurately, only *desires* to know truth.

In this sense, it is misleading to speak of Indian thought as a *philosophy*. It is, rather, an *investigation* into reality, with the full intention of accepting only as much as it can actually prove to be true. It is not the mere love of wisdom; it is *sophia*: It is wisdom itself.

Serious investigation may begin with the study of

known facts, but it proceeds from them, if possible to discover unknown, but knowable, marvels. Science certainly set an example of uninspired plodding when it closed the door on countless fascinating questions that it considered unanswerable. It refused to debate the immortality of the soul, or the existence of God, or whether iron can be transmuted into gold. Instead, it addressed itself to the few dull, but at least measurable, phenomena that seemed willing to surrender their humble secrets, as if grateful for a hearing at last. By resolute self-honesty, however, science has succeeded in probing reality to heretofore unimagined depths.

An accusation often leveled at Indian thought is that its focus is too subjective. This objection might indeed be valid, were it true that every man is unique—or, as Sartre proclaimed, "radically free" of all external influences, and of the desires and drives that shape the destinies of other human beings.

Thumbprints are unique; why not, then, Sartre would ask, personalities? Yet thumbprints have been categorized for the simple reason that the thumb itself is a common human appendage. Personalities, similarly, are unique, but only superficially so. There are levels of consciousness that all men share in common. Individual idiosyncrasies are only extensions of the basic humanity of every man. It is a mistake to think that, because of the complexity of human nature, it cannot be reduced to certain universal principles.

It may be pointed out here that material phenomena, too, are complex. Science has often had to struggle to reduce the bewildering array of factual data to universal principles.

It is a mistake to think that a subjectively arrived at insight cannot, by definition, be objectively valid. Most great discoveries, in science as well as in any other field, have come to their discoverers first as clear and incontrovertible intuitions. Indeed, even in science, distinctions of subjective and objective are rapidly disappearing.

Consider some of the mundane facts that are usually looked upon most confidently as objective realities: those aspects of nature which can be observed objectively.

These phenomena would never even have been noticed, had the early scientists not been actively searching for them, and had those men not been in some way prepared to find them.

The great physicist, Sir Arthur Eddington, put it this way:

Where Science has progressed the farthest, the mind has but regained from nature that which the mind has put into nature.

Indeed, it seems likely that the only certainty we shall ever abstract from the universe is our simple ability to *think* of abstracting something from it—that is to say, our ideas, our expectations.

What science tests, essentially, is the concepts it has already formed regarding the true nature of things. And what India's investigations sought to accomplish was to understand the factory from which all concepts come: human consciousness.

Here indeed may be found, besides concepts regarding external matters (which touch us less deeply as human beings), other concepts that touch us profoundly: the secret of happiness, for example; and how to achieve peace of mind; and the true basis of inner confidence. Admittedly, these matters cannot be reduced to statistics or to slide rule measurements, like the studies pursued by the physical sciences. Yet they compensate for their elusiveness by the fact of being more directly knowable, and more meaningful to us, in terms of actual human experience.

Westerners who have tried to understand human nature by following scientific methodology have taken the wrong cue from science. They have allowed its materialistic bias to influence them in a field that has little or nothing to do with matter. It should be obvious that non-material subjects need to be studied on their own ground. Instead, however, these self-proclaimed scientists have confined their interest to more or less physical tests. When studying moral principles, for example, their approach has been statistical. As well might a jeweler measure the carats of a gem stone with a snow shovel; or a literary critic determine the genius of Shakespeare by listening to the applause of yokels.

The investigations of India, unbiased by scientific materialism, were conducted in that field where one would more naturally expect such investigations to be carried out: in the consciousness of man. They entailed a search for personal fulfillment, and not for techniques of mass conditioning or manipulation. Above all, they were rooted in common sense, not in elaborate intellectual theories.

The electron, J.W.N. Sullivan wrote, is the key to the

universe. Individual man, similarly, as we saw in Chapter Two, must provide the key to unlocking the secrets of human nature.

The investigations of India's seers would prove merely subjective if the doors they'd unlocked gave entrance only to their own specific natures. What their approach accomplished, instead, was to unlock doors to universal aspects of human nature.

India's investigations did begin with certain rather commonplace observations. But this is what science did, also. The child must learn to walk before it can run.

This question of relativism, for example: Nothing, really, could be more obvious than the fact that values are in fact relative. This truth stares us in the face every day of our lives.

Who worries, for example, when a child plays at shooting people with a toy gun? Again, it doesn't strike us as infamous for a soldier to kill in defense of his country. The little child is not expected to understand adult moral standards. And the soldier's duty is to fight in his country's defense.

To speak of non-killing, then, as a categorical imperative is obviously possible only in the abstract. Rather than wish things otherwise in an effort to fit them to some preconceived notion of what morality means, it makes more sense to do what India did: observe the facts as they relate to different levels of life experience, and then work from there.

India's investigations into the nature of man addressed not, at first, the grand, cosmic mysteries, but rather the simple questions, matters of more immediate human concern. They derived their axioms, not from an idealized or theoretical picture of human nature, but, again, from simple, easily repeatable experiments— experiments that were subjective, inasmuch as they involved self-observation, but that were objective as well, inasmuch as they penetrated to levels of reality that were not unique to them as individuals, but universally true for all human beings.

Always, the emphasis was on proof—the proof of workability, of direct experience. Reason, as I've pointed out, was kept in a secondary and supportive role; it was not looked to to direct the process. Assertions were made on the basis of carefully observed and analyzed experience. They never took the form, however, of categorical dogmas. Students were told to accept a teaching only as an exercise in understanding, until such time as they, too, had carefully tested it and proved to their own satisfaction that it worked.

Because the assertions of Indian thought concern matters of universal experience, they deserve a respect that is reserved, presently, for scientific discoveries alone. For as science looks behind the facade of diversity in life to discover unifying principles, so Indian thought, similarly, probes beneath the waves of individual idiosyncrasies to find realities that are common to all mankind.

CHAPTER EIGHT

Truth in Relativity
Part II

DIRECTIONAL RELATIVITY

INDIA'S INVESTIGATIONS into the nature of reality were essentially man-oriented, not matter-oriented. The first questions asked of the universe concerned animate, not inanimate, matter, and focused more particularly on the attributes of consciousness.

It is interesting to note that psychologists, sociologists, and others who deal with human problems have paid little attention to science's present view of a non-material, and more especially a non-mechanical, universe. These would-be scientists have followed traditional science in its materialism. They have measured, weighed, timed, categorized, and codified to exhaustion, but not particularly to anyone's enlightenment.

We have seen that certain mental attitudes produce inner tension, and, consequently, unhappiness in the individual. Western social scientists would probably insist that no such claim should be made until a prolonged study had been conducted of some hundreds or thousands of people. Even then, they wouldn't expect any of their colleagues to be so bold as to announce a *discovery*. He must announce tentative findings, "pending further study."

Albert A. Michelson and Edward Morley were able with a single experiment to shake the world of physics. Sociologists, by contrast, feel that they must repeat their experiments endlessly to command even a hearing. To strengthen their credentials among what they are pleased to think of as their fellow scientists, they attempt to treat man as essentially an object, viewing him always as something "wholly other" than themselves.

In so doing, they find themselves competing at a disadvantage with the material sciences. For while it is possible, in controlled experiments in the laboratory, to establish conditions where material phenomena behave uniformly, no such possibility exists for the study of human behavior. The variables in humanity, viewed, anyway, in terms of outward behavior, are simply too numerous.

To try to arrive at common denominators of behavior, social scientists are obliged to work with statistics. If enough people report feelings, let us say, of unhappiness under tension, they may conclude—always tentatively, of course—that a corollary *seems* to exist between tension and unhappiness. Even then, the question will remain open as to whether tension is the *cause* of unhappiness, or the *effect* of it; whether extraneous factors such as social conditioning are at work also; and whether, indeed, so vague a word as *unhappiness* can ever be defined comprehensively enough to be considered "clinically meaningful."

Statistics of human behavior can no doubt be fascinating. Occasionally they are even helpful. Essentially, however, the statistical approach to human nature is a stopgap measure, a desperate tactic employed for want of anything better. It represents an effort to salvage *something,* at least, of scientific methodology, and thereby to maintain before the world the illusion that the statisticians, too, merit all the respect that is given nowadays to scientists generally.

Yet everyone knows that human behavior cannot really be categorized so conveniently. The statistic may indeed be the only scientific method for arriving at facts of human nature that are even moderately useful. Of all methods, however, it is probably, even in the material sciences, the least satisfactory because generally the least conclusive.

It seems foolish in any case to insist on applying a mere fragment of orthodox methodology to the study of man—of all phenomena by far the most complex. What we need, rather, is to seek alternatives to that methodology in a system more obviously adapted to the subject. Neither modern science nor conceptual logic have shown themselves capable of pursuing this study more deeply than the superficiality of statistics, or than the untested assumptions with which all of us are familiar.

India, on the other hand, presents us not only with profound conclusions, but with a methodology as well for arriving at those conclusions ourselves.

Of particular interest is the fact that, on application,

this new system turns out to be not so radically different, after all, from that of modern science.

The scientist, in order to get at the nature of an element, doesn't bother to make an exhaustive survey of the various forms that have been assumed by that element. He tries, rather, to get down into the element itself—to study, perhaps, the components of a single one of its atoms.

If one were to take up the study of man without prior familiarity with scientific methodology, this, probably, is the approach he would take: He would make an *in depth* study of man, the individual. In fact, in so doing he could not be accused of being unscientific. The essential difference between the study of matter and the study of man would lie only in the fact that man is not a chemical element, and must be studied in a way that is appropriate to what he is.

To approach human nature only from the outside, as sociologists do with their statistics, is to commit oneself to superficiality. A broad study of thousands of people is bound to be trivial. The more in-depth the study, on the other hand, the more significant it will be.

India's ancient seers found that the best way for anyone to get to the core of human nature is simply this: *for man to make a deep study of his own nature.* This, as we know, was the insight also behind the ancient Greek dictum: "Know thyself."

Objective self-study doesn't have to mean seeing oneself as others see him—from without, in other words. It can and should especially mean examining *without personal prejudice* one's own thought processes, in order to penetrate the countless layers of subconscious rationalization.

This task is so difficult that it may in fact require help from another person (a role played in India by the wise guru). Without such an approach, however, it is difficult to see how human nature could ever be understood at its depths. One cannot dissect consciousness with a surgeon's knife. Our understanding of other people depends entirely upon our depth of self-understanding. To see others objectively, moreover, requires first of all an ability to be objective with oneself.

For these reasons, Indian philosophy is introspective, and very rightly so. It claims, moreover, that self-study (*swadhyaya,* in the Sanskrit), if carried deeply enough, penetrates beneath the idiosyncrasies of human nature to reveal universals.

Our social scientists cannot begin to argue this point; they have not made the effort even to get under the skin of their subject, what to speak of trying, like the physicists, to get to its heart. *A priori* assumptions have always stood in their way.

It is an interesting fact that all those in India's history who have conducted this in-depth *swadhyaya* have encountered the same universals. Remember, these people represented the highest and best of their civilization: the independent thinkers, the iconoclasts and trailblazers, the men and women who opposed the needless strictures of orthodoxy. They were people like Buddha, who dared to challenge even the authority of the *Veda*s—or, more accurately, who challenged the orthodox priests in their interpretations of that authority.

Those brave souls were the "new wineskins" (to use an expression made famous by Jesus Christ), who appear in every age and nation, and by whom alone the world is inspired to accept new ideas. Nothing but relentless self-honesty led them to the conclusions they reached. It was the accuracy of those conclusions, and not the orthodoxy of their philosophical stance, that brought them into harmony with other great men and women before them. Their unanimity is a testimony to the universality of their insights, and not to any unquestioning orthodoxy of their dogmas.

Often, indeed—as often happens to great souls—they found themselves persecuted by the orthodox of their day, who, being superficial themselves, could not understand the scriptures except superficially.

The best way to get the right answers is to ask the right questions. In the study of man, the right questions concern those things which most deeply affect man himself, and not such secondary questions as those the sociologists ask.

One such essential question would surely be: "What does man want from life?" This is, in fact, one of the starting points of Indian philosophy. A simple enough question, too; it is comparable to one of the earliest questions asked by science: "What makes the planets move as they do?" In the case of the planets, Kepler was forced to assume mechanical causes; one can't ask a planet, after all, to explain its reasons for behaving as it does. In the case of man, however, we are not hindered by any such "communication gap"; man can speak for himself.

What does man want from life? Better still, what do

we want from life? For we needn't study the desires of thousands of other people; the sheer diversity of our own desires is already bewildering, and self-contradictory, enough! The answer to our question in any case will not be found in some desire of the moment. Nor will it lie in some more long-range, but still superficial, desire for a house, a stable income, or a flower garden. These are only manifestations of deeper needs of human nature. We may want a house and a stable income, for example, because of an underlying desire for security. But then again we must ask: Why do I want security?

India's researchers into human motivation, following the thread of desire to its source, found that man's deepest motivation is essentially this: to avoid suffering, and to attain happiness. And while suffering and happiness have different meanings for different people, their basic reality is the same for all.

This observation was given the weight of a formal law of human nature: *Beneath every sensory desire is the deeper urge to avoid pain, and to experience pleasure; and beneath every deeper, heart's desire is the longing to escape sorrow, and to attain permanent happiness, or joy.*

This law proved to be as basic to further explorations in consciousness as Newton's laws of motion were to the further development of physics. The motivational law, indeed, like those of modern science, carried its first basic perception to a view of reality that is not only expansive, but cosmic.

This law, according to our Western traditions, deserves a name. Let us, accordingly, name it, the *Law of Motivation.* And let us consider how the ancient sages proceeded to apply this *Law of Motivation* to the question of moral principles.

If the goal of every man is to avoid suffering and attain happiness, then the eternal question of moral right and wrong can be decided quite simply by this criterion. What makes an act right? The answer: its capacity to increase happiness. And what makes an act wrong? The answer, again: its power to lessen happiness, and to increase suffering.

One can imagine Sartre rubbing his hands at this point and shouting, "Comrades!" For since the search must be into the heart of *one* human being, right and wrong must resolve themselves into the more specific question: "What will decrease suffering, and increase happiness, *for me?*" Sartre would be premature in his exultation, however. The *Law of Motivation* in no way counsels a cynical view.

It might be added that cynicism, with its implied bias, can play no part in any honest investigation. A truly impartial observer is determined to see things as they are, regardless of the implications.

If, then, I accept as my premise that, to understand human nature fully, I must begin with a study of myself, I cannot afford to back off shamefacedly before the obvious corollary to this approach: self-centeredness. Prejudice is a stumbling block in any scrupulous search for truth. Rather, I must pursue this issue of self-centeredness with an open mind and let it lead me where it will.

In fact, as we shall soon see, the desire for personal happiness can be truly fulfilled only when it includes the happiness of all; and the desire to avoid suffering can be fulfilled, similarly, only when one works to help eliminate the sorrows of all.

Let us address the issue squarely. Can any system based so completely on self-fulfillment be meaningful in a broader, humanitarian sense? Addressing the bias of Western moralism, is not a self-centered approach to happiness morally reprehensible?

An ethics of self-fulfillment might seem at first glance to encourage grabbing whatever one can at the expense of everyone else. "Looking out for number one" is an expression one hears rather too often nowadays.

I remember seeing a cartoon of a little old lady embroidering the motto, "Look after number one," on an old-fashioned wall-hanging. The joke of the cartoon was the incongruity of someone in old age harboring the competitive and selfish drive of a young opportunist (usually male) trying to elbow his way upwards aggressively in the world. And what's so funny about that? Simply that, on some level of our consciousness, we all assume that ego-centricity will lose some of its rough edges as we grow older and, hopefully, wiser.

Man always wants more, not less, happiness than he has already. He errs, however, when he thinks he can increase his happiness by adding to his possessions rather than by expanding his awareness. Any effort to increase his happiness without at the same time expanding his sensitivity to the world around him, and his sense of identity with it, will be self-defeating. Whenever a person acts selfishly, he deadens the capacity, inherent in every human being, to perceive his essential unity with all life. He becomes, as a result, petty and mean.

The expansion of happiness necessarily entails the expansion of awareness, not the expansion of property. For happiness is not a thing, and cannot be found in mere things. It is a quality of consciousness: something that one is aware *with,* rather than *of.*

Reason therefore suggests, *and inner experience confirms,* that happiness is an intrinsic quality of human nature. We enjoy things only to the extent that we satisfy the thought in our own minds that things are enjoyable. In fact, it is never things themselves that we enjoy at all, but only a deeper reality within our own being.

George Bernard Shaw expressed a deep truth—with no intention, one suspects, of being profound—when, seated one evening outside the circle of a party, he was approached by his hostess and asked if he was enjoying himself. Glaring at her from under his bushy eyebrows, he replied, "That's all I am enjoying!"

The clearest proof that things are not enjoyable *in themselves* may be seen in the fact that different people can have such very different ideas as to what gives them happiness. I had this point emphasized for me one day in Los Angeles. I had accepted a ride downtown with a neighbor in his car. It was a beautiful morning, and I made some conventional remark about the weather. To my surprise, the man replied with a snarl: "This damn sun! For twenty years I've been living in Southern California and I've seen nothing but sunshine. I'm sick to death of it!" There we were, experiencing the same weather, but for one of us the experience was a happy one, and for the other, a miserable one!

The desire to attain happiness is actually symptomatic of the desire for *self*-discovery, for *self*-fulfillment. By the same token, the desire to avoid suffering is essentially a desire to eschew "non-happiness" as foreign to our nature. We suffer only when something withholds from us that degree of happiness which we feel to be rightfully ours.

We suffer also from the limitations we place on our own happiness. Consider this example:

You are walking cheerfully down the street, delighted with life. The birds in the trees are all singing, the sun is shining; everything seems haloed in a magical light. All at once, glancing into a store window, you behold a coat that perfectly matches your morning mood. And suddenly you think, "I've simply *got* to have it!" It's expensive, unfortunately, and you haven't the money to buy it.

Now the sunlight doesn't seem quite so bright anymore, nor the birds' songs so beautiful. You feel that, to enjoy your happy mood *perfectly,* you simply must have that coat.

Your own thoughts, you see, have placed a limitation on your happiness—just as, by fulfilling that desire, you will *think* yourself back to your former happy mood once again.

Suffering, quite as much so as gladness, is in the mind. When at last you find yourself able to buy that coat of your dreams, you will not so much *increase* your happiness as remove the restriction that you placed on it in the first place.

Multiply that desire by thousands, perhaps even millions, of other unfulfilled desires, most of them buried long ago in your subconscious mind, and you have the root cause of all human sorrow and bondage.

The expansion of happiness is not so much an increase as a *return* to our normal state of being.

The same also is true of the expansion of awareness. Self-realization doesn't mean egoistically cutting oneself off from the universe and from one's fellow man. It means, rather, an increasing realization of one's essential *identity* with others and with ever-broader realities. Generosity to others, far from contradicting one's instinct for self-fulfillment, affirms it and more deeply satisfies it.

It must be clear by now that Indian ethics is not so offensive to the sensibilities of Western moralists as may have at first appeared. In fact, the two systems of morality are, in their actual formulations, so markedly similar that one suspects they were born of the same insights.

Is it possible that the commandments of Moses were, originally, less formidable than they seem to us, haloed as they have become in absolutism? Is it possible, in other words, that they were attuned to human welfare, and not merely to human governance?

Jesus Christ said, "The Sabbath was made for man, and not man for the Sabbath." This statement is in keeping with the Indian approach to moral values. The main difference, in fact, between the Indian and the Western systems of ethics lies in the incentives they normally offer. Where Western ethics commonly urges men to be kind, forgiving, and otherwise virtuous in denial of their basic nature, Indian ethics urges these same virtues as the deeper fulfillment of that nature.

There is a second, and equally important, point to be considered on this subject. We have established that moral values exist, and that they are deeply rooted in human nature. Let us now ask whether it is possible, within the framework of relativism, for universal values to exist.

If the *Law of Motivation* lies at the basis of moral values, then we must accept morality as a *developing guideline,* and not as an absolute commandment, since happiness itself is a fluid, not a fixed, condition. One can, in other words, be more happy, or less so, rather than *either* happy *or* miserable.

And this, from the standpoint of the despair of modern thinkers in their confrontation with relativity, constitutes perhaps the most important contribution of Indian thought.

For, obviously, the relativity of happiness is no one's cause for confusion. In referring to our inner feelings, we wouldn't say, "Well, speaking personally I'd say I was in a state of sheer euphoria, but I can't say that I'd be justified in doing so, because I don't know what it would look like to the tribesmen of Borneo." We don't define our own happiness, in other words, by relating it to a multitude of other opinions as to what happiness is.

Our social philosophers have tried to do that with the question of morality. Even they, however, would define happiness quite simply, if at all, in terms of itself: "Am I more happy, or less so, than I was before?"

The same guideline applies, according to this way of thinking, to the question of values. *The relativity of values is directional.*

Western ethics accepts only grudgingly the obvious fact that man cannot become perfectly moral in one step. By the standards of Western rational absolutism, anything that falls short of morality as it is authoritatively defined must, by very definition, be *im*moral. Western man has therefore always lived in the long shadow of the belief that, no matter how hard he tries, he is much more likely to offend God than to please Him.

The inevitable corollary to this depressing belief is the so-called "Protestant ethic"—the feeling that duty must always be grimly unpleasant.* Indeed, if perfection is impossibly out of reach, and if any state short of perfection represents failure, then every "commandment" to be good becomes merely a discouraging reminder of how utterly bad one really is. The discouragement is only increased when moral duty is urged in opposition to human nature.

What joy can there possibly be in attempting an impossible task with the sure knowledge that the punishment for failure will be absolute—indeed, eternal? Small wonder that Christians are so often prone to let Jesus do the worrying about their condition after death, while they live as they more or less please here on earth—going to church, perhaps, once a week or so to

* A singer of my acquaintance was once recording a few songs with me in a studio. At one point she exclaimed, "I'm really enjoying myself!" But then she added doubtfully, "But that makes me feel guilty. It always seems to me somehow wrong to enjoy what I'm doing, when I'm trying to be conscientious about it!"

reassure him that they still believe in him, and to remind him that they still hold him to his side of the bargain.

Indian ethics is more pragmatic. Basing its view of morality squarely on the question of human fulfillment, and not on abstract definitions of what is morality, it admits of a *growth* towards perfection.

This approach is completely consonant with natural law. In this sense, it is much more rational than the rigid categories of Western rationalism. Is it not better, after all, to encourage a baby to crawl than to scold it because it can't run? As the Bhagavad Gita puts it: "Even the wise man acts according to the tendencies of his own nature. All living beings go according to their natures. What can mere suppression avail?" (III:33)

Indian ethics, submitting as it does to the test of experience, is made actually *more* coherent by the doctrine of relativism. For relativism, in the Indian sense, suggests directional development, and not directionless confusion.

We come here to a question that is vitally important for the relevance of the *Law of Motivation* to the issue of ethics: Can *universal* guidelines of behavior be developed out of the Indian system, introspective and relativistic as it is?

One may tell people that, to expand their happiness, they must think more of others and less selfishly of themselves. To bring this teaching down to specific guidelines, however, may be more difficult.

Western ethics is presented as a system of absolute principles, which one is expected to "follow, or else." In a system of ethics, however, where subjective fulfillment is the guideline, it is clear that specific rules cannot be so categorical. If they demanded more of a person than he was prepared, by his own level of maturity, to follow, they might bring him the very opposite of self-fulfillment. A truly generous person, for example, might find joy (as St. Francis did) in giving away his last possession to a beggar. A selfish person, on the other hand, might suffer acutely in being forced to give away even his second piece of cake.

There are degrees of maturity. The rules must necessarily change according to the degree. Action that too far outstrips a person's actual understanding may result only in frustration; certainly it will not result in meaningful growth. That is why the Bhagavad Gita says, "In doing the activity appointed to one's own state of being, one does not acquire any fault." (XVIII:47)

India's ancient seers laid down guidelines for the main stages in human growth toward spiritual maturity. Specifically, this growth was outlined in the four *ashramas*, or stages of life, and again in the four social castes.

The caste system originally was not based on heredity, as it has come to be interpreted in recent centuries. It was meant not as an instrument of social repression, but as a general guideline to *inner* development and Self-realization. It was the individual, by his own temperament, who determined to what caste he belonged. Implicit in the system was always the possibility of a person developing to a point where he naturally belonged in a higher caste, or, conversely, degenerating to a point where he belonged in a lower.

For just as an individual experiences many different

degrees of awareness in the course of his lifetime, so also are varying levels of awareness a feature of society at large.

It is popular nowadays to claim that all men are equal. Yet, whatever equality they may share before God, it would be naive to insist that all men are equally intelligent, equally talented, or equally mature. Amusingly, the same society that clings so fervently to this delusion of universal equality proclaims loudly the relativity of everything else in the universe!

People of the lowest order of refinement were designated in ancient India as *Sudra*s—the kind of person, that is to say, whose awareness is so dull that creative (i.e. expansive) thought is virtually nonexistent for him. The *Sudra* is the type of individual whose purely automatic responses brand him as a perennial effect in life, never a cause: the sort who, nowadays, spends all his free time in front of a television set, and accepts only the ideas that are given to him at prime time, challenging nothing except as he is, perhaps, programmed to challenge.

To ask such a person to think creatively would be unrealistic. It is enough to ask of him that he not be totally inert; that he exert himself at least physically, and thereby develop, if only on a level of body-awareness, a measure of dignity and pride in the fact of his humanity.

In ancient times, *Sudra*-types were encouraged to work with their hands, to avoid sloth, and—by serving an employer more creatively aware than themselves—to try to absorb something of his creative spark.

People in whom the creative spark (i.e., the spirit of self-expansion) was alive, but not yet refined enough to reach out sympathetically to others, were recognized as belonging to the next stage up the ladder of human development. They were called *Vaisya*s, and were epitomized as merchants.

Typically, the *Vaisya*-type nowadays is the sort of person who devotes all his energy to "making a fast buck." He is clever. He possesses initiative and an abundance of energy and ingenuity. All this energy and ingenuity, however, is devoted to "looking out for number one."

It would be as unrealistic to ask such a person to devote himself to social upliftment as to ask a *Sudra*-type to think creatively. *Vaisya*s in ancient India were therefore encouraged to be creative while they worked for themselves, and thereby (on a level of intelligence, as opposed to mere brawn) to develop a sense of dignity and pride in their own humanity. At the same time they were urged, if only by appeals to their vanity, to become useful and responsible members of society. For at this stage of development it is usually necessary to approach people through their self-interest. Only thus may it be possible to get them to think of others' welfare at all.

With the further refinement of awareness, activity from motives of self-aggrandizement becomes understood *from within oneself* to be unworthy of the true purpose and dignity of man. Such activity is then seen no longer as self-expansive, but as self-limiting.

At this stage of development, a person finds himself ready to stop pampering his ego, and reaches out instinctively in sympathy to help others. At this stage, then, he needs progressively to renounce self-seeking, and is urged to seek his fulfillment in helping others, or in service to some high ideal.

Those people in ancient times who had reached this stage of development were called *Kshatriya*s, and were epitomized as warriors, or as leaders in society—as people, that is to say, who were ready to dedicate themselves to the welfare of others, and even, if necessary, to lay down their lives in a high cause.

Properly speaking, the *Kshatriya* is one who is ready to understand *by inner feeling,* and not by outer precept alone, that happiness and self-fulfillment are entirely states of mind; that they depend not on accumulating mere things, but on expanding one's awareness and identity to embrace the welfare of all.

Even the *Kshatriya* state, however, noble though it is, falls short of the perfection that is humanity's highest potential. It is a transition, only, from thing-centeredness to bliss-centeredness. The *Kshatriya*-type does what he can for the welfare of others, and for his own inner growth. Sooner or later, however, he reaches a point in his development where he discovers (again, by inner feeling, and not by mere outer precept) that to serve people outwardly is not so important for them, nor so satisfying for himself, as to help them to find inner joy, through an expansion of awareness.

He becomes, then, no longer the warrior or dedicated public servant, but the spiritual teacher: the *Brahmin.* Ideally, in this highest calling, he comes to recognize that teaching others is in itself not enough, and that the best way to uplift others is to remain always immersed in inner bliss. Thus, his very teaching becomes, as he develops progressively, primarily a sharing of consciousness, more so even than a sharing of ideas.

These four stages of human development may be compared to a bar magnet, in which the respective positions of north and south are always relative to each other, but always directionally so. No matter where, or in how many pieces, a bar magnet is divided, each of the resulting fragments maintains its own north-south polarity. Even at the northernmost end, the molecules will have their south as well as their north polarity. And even at the southernmost end, the molecules will maintain their north polarity.

Within each of the four castes, similarly, gradations may be found that represent the entire sequence. The most developed *Sudras* are *Brahmin*-like in relation to other *Sudras*; and the least developed *Brahmins* are *Sudra*-like compared to other *Brahmins*.

The true relativity of human values is their directional alignment with inner human development. At every stage of that development, those attitudes which point in the direction of further growth are "good," because self-fulfilling; and those which point in the opposite direction are "bad" for the simple reason that they take one away from what he himself truly wants, which is an increase of happiness, and into what he does not want, which is suffering.

What is morally good and right at one stage of development becomes bad at a more advanced stage.

Consider this example: Suppose a Jesus Christ or a Mahatma Gandhi were to awaken one morning and shout, "I'm tired of serving humanity. From now on I'm going to go out and work and become a millionaire." Wouldn't everyone, even the most worldly, exclaim, "This man has fallen!"?

But then suppose someone whom everyone considered almost pathetically lazy were to get up one morning from his bed of ease and announce, "I'm going to go out and work and become a millionaire." Wouldn't even the most spiritually minded people exclaim, "Good for him!"?

It is not so easy as one would like to advance always toward the good, even though in this direction alone lie personal fulfillment and happiness, while in the other lies personal pain. For the remembered pleasures at lower stages of development often interpose themselves, tempting one to reverse his footsteps. Negativity, like the south pole of a magnet, has its own attractive power. That is why emphasis at every stage of development should be on self-expansion, and not on self-gratification; on service, and not on being served.

The steps on the path of inner development are relative not only to each other, but also to the ultimate goal of the journey, which is perfect joy. On the way to that goal, each stage of the journey is the same for everyone at that particular point. The rules of behavior at that stage, then, apply universally to all of them, even if those rules are not necessarily valid for those at other stages along the way. And while it is incorrect to say that values are absolute, it is perfectly correct to say that, in their directional relativity, they are universal.

A man may not, in other words, use the fact of relativism whimsically to invent his own private code of behavior. While it is true that his own needs will not be the needs of all, and that what is right for him to do is not necessarily right for another, these facts do not imply that right and wrong are matters of personal opinion. There is a direction in which all human beings must move, if they would fulfill the basic law of their own being.

Failure to cooperate with this universal law only means increasing in oneself the inharmony, and the sense of insufficiency and limitation, that furnish man his constant prod to move forward. At whatever point one now stands, he must put his next foot forward on the path, not backwards or sideways, if he would fulfill his own innate drive for greater happiness, awareness, and freedom of consciousness.

Relativity has been used by modern writers to justify a philosophy of meaninglessness. Relativism derives much of its power from the discovery that, apart from the constant speed of light, no fixed realities exist anywhere that can serve as points of reference for determining anything. Who could say, absolutely, that a planet is moving fast or slowly, up or down, forward or backward; that it is large or small, light or heavy? Always the same question would arise: large, small, light, or heavy with reference to *what?*

In a cosmic sense these questions are actually meaningless. Assuming that our sun and another star appear to be moving toward each other, this could be an illusion. We would not really know whether our sun was moving toward that star, or away from it. The mere fact of diminishing distance could be easily explained by saying that we are moving away from it more slowly than it is overtaking us. There is even the intriguing possibility that, in a spherical universe, what looks in one direction like a drawing together might be seen as a drawing apart, viewed in other directions.

The question of good and evil, similarly, has come these days to be considered meaningless because people see it as related to matters of social convenience, and not rooted in absolute truth. India's definition of good and evil, born of the *Law of Motivation,* derives from relating good to an ultimate purpose of life, and evil, to the negation of that purpose.

If the relativity of values is true, then there must be truth in that relativity, and truth and relativism must therefore support one another. In fact, as we have seen, this is what they do.

The directional relativity that we have discovered in human development, and therefore in human values, calls for a very different kind of thinking from the categorical reasoning that has so long dominated Western thought. In the old system in the West, a thing was either good or bad. In most modern efforts to adjust to an Einsteinian universe, things have been considered basically neither good nor bad. In a system of directional relativity, however, a meaningless "neither/nor" becomes transformed into a highly meaningful "both/and."

At the very farthest extremities of evil, some aspect of human nature cannot but face in the direction of greater goodness, just as in a bar magnet the molecules at the southernmost end maintain their north pole as well. Instead of calling everything at the dark end of human nature *evil,* we may rightly call the "north pole" of even our worst qualities at least relatively *good.* Instead of abandoning ourselves to despair whenever we fall into error, we should realize that in every state of consciousness, no matter how debased, there is a better as well as a worse side, and that the better side represents actual goodness at that stage of development.

Sin then is, quite simply, error. And virtue is the positive aspect of error quite as much as it is, in its own right, a conscious and deliberate flow towards truth.

The challenge of relativism to life's meaning, when seen in this light, becomes no challenge at all, but a corroboration of meaning.

At least we have found this to be so in the consideration of human values. But what about a broader perspective? Is the directional relativity we have discovered so far a uniquely human phenomenon? Have we abstracted meaning from this relative universe by merely fencing human experience off from the rest of reality? What about the seeming accident of evolution? What about the material basis of life and consciousness? And what about the claim of biologists that there has been no meaningful progress in evolution?

In the next four chapters we'll extend the approach we have developed so far, to explore some of the broader realities by which modern science seems to have undermined humanity's sense of ultimate meaning. In so doing, I think the reader will discover with me that relativity here, too, only *deepens* our overall sense that we are living in a richly meaningful universe.

CHAPTER NINE

Meaning in Evolution?
Part I

If relativity on a human level is directional and pro-gressive, why has no such directional development been discerned in the evolution of life up to the human level? Reputable biologists generally consider natural evolution to have been quite purposeless, directionless, and accidental.

Has there been an actual evolution of life? That is to say, has evolution been progressive? Or has there been nothing but a continuous process of change?

Examining the evidence amassed by biologists, but reinterpreting it in the light of the experience of individual animals—rather than, more vaguely, of entire species—it becomes clear that there is an intel-ligent direction in the whole evolutional scheme.

CHAPTER NINE

Meaning in Evolution?
Part I

The floating heads with their starveling bodies,
the squid which emitted clouds of luminescent
ink and vanished in their own bright explosions,
were all a part of one of life's strongest quali-
ties—its eternal dissatisfaction with what is, its
persistent habit of reaching out into new envi-
ronments and, by degrees, adapting itself to the
most fantastic circumstances.
　　　—Loren Eiseley, in *The Immense Journey*

IT IS NOT MY PURPOSE in this volume to enter deeply into a discussion of Indian philosophy, but only to consider those points at which it touches meaningfully on certain widespread dilemmas of our times. Most specifically, I have considered the problem of meaninglessness.

Nowhere has the case for meaninglessness been made so strongly as in the study of evolution. If the majority of modern biologists are right, evolution—indeed, the very appearance of life on this planet—has been completely accidental. In this view, the only hope of man's finding any meaning in life lies in isolating himself from the rest of nature, in looking for purely human meanings. But to exclude man from nature is to overlook the natural—which is to say, the reality—in man. To do so leads inevitably back to an affirmation of meaninglessness, through an emphasis on merely invented, rather than discovered, values.

It is necessary, in any meaningful discussion of human values, to keep the door open between man and the objective universe of which he is so integrally a part. If there is a chance that nature, apart from man, really is meaningless, it will simply not do for us to look vaguely the other way and go on talking earnestly about meaning in *human* life.

Keeping in mind the directional relativity that we discussed in the last chapter, let us take a long, hard look at this whole question of meaning in evolution, and see whether it refutes or supports our thesis of an ethic rooted in natural law.

What is evolution? How does it take place?

Let us begin with that friendly old question: How did the leopard get its spots? Did the animal *want* spots, and evolve them deliberately? Again, was there an intention in the mind of a Creator that leopards should be spotted? Or—a third alternative—did the spots merely happen?

Vitalists claim that the leopard wanted its spots. The second possibility, that the usefulness of spots to the leopard suggests that it got them by divine plan, is the argument advanced by *Finalists. Materialists* champion the third alternative, that the spots simply happened. *Vitalism, finalism,* and *materialism*—these are the three best-known viewpoints on heredity.

Of the three, most modern biologists subscribe to the third. Nowadays, the serious student of evolution is almost obliged by the alternatives as they've been presented to become materialistic.

How *did* the leopard get its spots? Biologists claim that they happened by a process of natural selection. The start of the process was accidental: a mutation that resulted in a spotted cub being born into what may have been a spotless breed.

Mutations are constantly occurring in nature. Most of them, biologists note, are disadvantageous. So would these spots have been, if this freakish cub had been born in the plains. It would have been quickly seen and avoided by any possible prey. It could not have lived so handsomely or so long as unspotted cats; the new strain, owing to its natural handicap, would have been gradually weeded out, following Darwin's well-substantiated law of survival.

As it happened, however, this particular cub was born in a jungle. Its spots gave it a decided advantage over its brothers and sisters. It could hunt more easily. It lived longer. It bore more offspring. Its spotted offspring, again, had a natural advantage over their unspotted brothers and sisters. Thus, gradually, the spotted jungle cats grew more numerous than their fellows. In time, they replaced those unfortunate misfits.

This is not merely a plausible theory. It has been substantiated in numerous ways. Man has brought about similar changes, for instance in dogs, by a process of deliberate selection. He has bred those dogs which had traits that he considered desirable, and has kept apart those with undesirable traits. Thus he has evolved completely new breeds, to which fact the great variety sharing our lives today bear ample witness. Natural selection functions in a very similar manner, the only real difference being that, for lack of deliberate selection and segregation, it takes much longer for such changes to become established.

So is the entire process of evolution explained.* Time was necessary, to be sure, to bring off the whole show. But then, time was one condition our planet could supply in abundance—two or three billion years of it, in fact, for the slow transformation of primeval protoplasm into the bewildering multiplicity that surrounds us today.

As biologists explain it, fish didn't decide to grow legs and lungs with a view to taking the fresh air. Random mutations occurred in this direction among various fishes, some of them, as it happened, living in shallow water. Bit by bit these shallow-water denizens came out onto dry land. Their legs and lungs grew, not because they willed them to grow, but simply because the longer-legged and bigger-lunged specimens stood a better chance of survival in the new environment, and had more opportunity to reproduce; thus, quite accidentally, they directed the evolution of land animals.

Similarly, new forms of life appeared—reptiles,

---

* An excellent, indeed perhaps the best, book on the subject, replete with examples and carefully thought-out arguments, is George Gaylord Simpson's *The Meaning of Evolution* (Yale University Press, New Haven, Conn., 1949).

insects, birds, mammals. It wasn't always, Simpson notes, a simple struggle for survival. But it was undeniably a process of progressive adaptation—that is, of entering and filling the slots available—not of deliberate previous intention. Simpson may even have meant to offer adaptation as a concession, however fleeting and casual, to intelligence. Simpson's bias is essentially mechanistic.

Now, in addition to these fairly clear facts we are told that no intelligent plan is evident in the process. To support this plea, Simpson (representing the majority of modern biologists) points out that many natural opportunities were never seized at all. Many changes were not the best imaginable under the circumstances.* Many innovations proved to be unfortunate, and failed. Regarding these, Simpson wrote: "If—the finalist reply—these are only sidelines that missed the goal, is it not impious to impute such fumbling to the Planner?"[†] (This is, of course, a very human conception of "the Planner." It is not to be gainsaid, however, that nature offers no obvious clues to the existence of such a Person.)

Simpson concludes: "The results of mutations do not tend to correspond at all closely with the needs or opportunities of the mutating organisms."[‡]

The only reason, then, according to him, for the

---

* Simpson shows an array of different kinds of antelopes, each with its own distinctive style of horns, none of them, perhaps, horns "that would have been mechanically the best, that an engineer would have chosen." (p. 167) It might be argued, of course, that mechanical perfection is not the only valid consideration—that esthetics, for instance, may play a role. But this objection can be countered effectively on other grounds.

† Ibid., p. 201.

‡ Ibid., p. 164.

wisdom life manifests so amazingly on every level is that, despite all this careless "fumbling," billions of years have made possible a few right answers to the twofold challenge of adaptation and survival. The entire process has been mechanical. There is no evidence anywhere of conscious direction, either from an inner vital force or from an omniscient Creator.

Irving Adler adds to this thought: "Nature is not like a breeder who purposely chooses the puppies that have traits that he likes. Nature chooses automatically and without purpose, as a result of the struggle for existence."*

Such, then, is the mechanistic point of view. Let us see whether this interpretation is the most logical one dictated by the facts themselves.

At the outset, it must be noted that a search for the mechanism of a thing is bound to reveal—well, what? Its mechanical functions, surely. Other considerations will simply not be pertinent to the subject at hand. Simpson wrote: "Scientists and particularly the professional students of evolution are often accused of a bias toward mechanism or materialism. . . . Such bias as may exist is inherent in the method of science."† Inherent, in other words, in its mechanistic orientation, which is almost like saying, in its bias—a perfect argument in a circle!

Simpson claims further that this scientific approach is, anyway, the least biased of human methodologies. Elsewhere, however, he admits: "Facts are elusive and you usually have to know what you are looking for

* Irving Adler, *How Life Began* (Signet Science Library Books, New York, 1959), p. 21.

† Op cit., p. 127.

before you can find one."* A materialistic approach is unlikely to discover, let alone to support, whatever nonmaterial realities there be.

Yet, if such an approach is honest, and if discrepancies exist that cannot be accounted for mechanistically, it is bound in time to discover them. At that time, a broader outlook will be seen to be necessary. Thus, physics has been forced virtually to abandon its old mechanistic outlook. If biology has not yet expanded its horizons to include nonmechanical realities, it can only be because it has not yet encountered the need to do so. It is still concerned with working out the mechanical aspects of its subject; it cannot yet afford the luxury of chasing through non-mechanistic mists.

That it will be forced to do so in time, however, goes almost without saying. If the most materially oriented of all sciences, physics, has had to admit the illusory nature of matter, it seems utterly improbable that biology, dealing as it does with living things, will continue indefinitely to think only in terms of chemistry and mechanical relationships. The very atoms of biochemistry are known now, in physics, to be but "another form of energy."†

But that a mechanistic explanation of evolution should be justifiable need not be surprising. The germ of the proof was already visible long ago, in the fact that no one stoops down from heaven to fashion individual trees. Trees grow from seeds, and produce seeds in their

---

* Ibid., p. 272.

† Harold F. Blum, in *Time's Arrow and Evolution.*

turn, to continue the process in more or less mechanical succession. Moreover, people have always known this process to be adaptive.

It is a matter of common observation that poor soil permits only the hardier trees to survive; that moist soil nurtures only those which can adapt to such moisture. It has always been recognized that only a successful tree will be able to perpetuate its line. (Dead trees don't produce blossoms.) These plain facts have been familiar to men for as far back as men have been developing trees. Should it be so surprising, then, that the mechanistic process has been found to extend backward in time beyond the tree?

To say, however, that the existence of the tree is explainable *solely* in terms of its mechanical genesis—this is quite another matter. To J.W.N. Sullivan, this proposition seemed a "stale and unlikely surmise."* To the thinking person it may seem as one-sided as it would be to claim that a great painting is nothing but a mixture of chemicals, or that a Bach organ fugue is nothing but wind finding its way out of various lengths of pipe.

As we see it, the difficulty boils down to an exaggerated emphasis on the *differences* between the accepted alternatives: vitalism, finalism and materialism. The real stumbling block is the thought that vitalism and finalism must be *super*-natural.

On careful thought, it should be clear that an absence of absolute wisdom in this relative, mundane scheme of things need not at all imply a complete

---

* J.W.N. Sullivan, *The Limitations of Science* (Mentor Books, New York, 1959), p. 186.

absence of intelligent, or at least of conscious, direction. Nescience is not the only alternative to omniscience.

Let us be specific. From a mechanistic point of view it is quite sufficient to say that the leopard got its spots by a process of natural selection, unspotted individuals gradually being weeded out by their comparative maladjustment to the jungle.

To deduce from this selective process, however, an absence of intelligent direction is to overlook the simple fact that the leopard is an intelligent animal.

An example of its intelligence is the skill with which it catches monkeys. If the monkeys elude its first charge, fleeing successfully to the treetops, the leopard may lie down on the ground and feign exhaustion or death. It knows the insatiable curiosity of the monkey tribe.

Sure enough, after awhile the monkeys descend slowly to the lower branches. After much chattering and jabbering among themselves, one of them may jump down to the ground to take a closer look. A bare two seconds later, it leaps back to arboreal safety.

The leopard is careful not to flicker an eyelid.

Presently, a monkey descends again to the ground, and creeps up cautiously to the leopard's tail—pulls it, perhaps, before scampering back in terror to the trees.

Still no movement from the wily predator.

At last, a monkey sneaks carefully around to the front of this sleeping mystery. It may reach out to tweak a tempting whisker. But curiosity is soon satisfied. Suddenly a lightning paw darts out; a jaw opens and snaps shut on a tasty morsel. A leopard has performed its Darwinian duty to survive yet another day.

The leopard is a hunter. Its stock of tricks is considerable. Everyone knows its skill, for example, in taking care to approach its prey from downwind. To assume that an unspotted leopard, maladjusted to the jungle, will simply sit around awaiting its doom is to take quite a lot for granted. Such a leopard will almost certainly head for the open spaces, where it is less likely to be seen. The spotted leopard, on the contrary, will make for the forest underbrush.

And what matter if the mechanics of the thing permit a leopard to will spots to its offspring or not? It has willed to make the best use of its own spots. For intelligent direction in evolution, nothing more than this personal, conscious adaptation to environment is necessary.

Again, in the choice of a mate it is entirely unnecessary to postulate something so improbable as a total lack of conscious selection. It can hardly be always so simple a matter as an "Oops, pardon me for bumping into you like this. Quite accidental, I assure you. Still, now that we've done it, perhaps we might as well breed?"

The spotty leopard will, other things being equal, choose for a mate another leopard with spots, one who can profitably share with him his jungle habitat. The fish that first takes a notion to stroll a bit on dry land will prefer a mate with similar inclinations. The freakish reptile with wings will prefer another one similarly endowed, if only as consolation for its own freakishness. Personal preference plays a definite role in sexual selection, as every naturalist will testify.

"But," someone will object, "even if environment and

a similar mate are selected, these are actions after the fact. The leopard had no say in developing those first spots. The deciding factor was a perfectly random mutation."

And yet, we reply, one of the chief symptoms of man's intelligence is his ability to make the best of available opportunities. Opportunities themselves very often come without his conscious effort. It is because he can utilize them to further his own ends, or change his ends to make better use of his opportunities, that his actions bear the mark of conscious direction.

Anyone who plodded blindly ahead in complete indifference to life's proffered opportunities would almost certainly be dubbed a fool. Yet—strange to say— this is the chief condition that writers have placed on heredity, for it to be intelligently directed!*

"But a breeder," it might be argued, "sets himself a definite goal when he tries to develop a new kind of dog. Nature, in its selections, reveals no such deliberation. The slightly spotted leopard isn't thinking of evolving a more spotted breed. The process may have in it an element of consciousness, but it has none of conscious direction toward a specific goal."

The catch here is that word, "goal." Even man is not so goal-oriented as he himself likes to make out (often after the event). A scientist often doesn't know towards what discoveries he is working. Yet he would feel himself insulted if anyone said that his work therefore lacks intelligent direction. It is enough that he is moving *for-*

---

* Simpson states that, "in the long quarrel between materialists and vitalists," this (to us peculiar) condition "has been recognized on both sides as a criterion." Op. cit., p. 129.

ward, deliberately seeking new answers to problems, new or old.

Even as a whole, science may not be said to have a goal, except in a directional sense. Many of its basic discoveries have been, in themselves, quite accidental—similar, if you like, to the mutations of Mendelian inheritance. Like those mutations, most of the facts turned up fortuitously in a laboratory are of no special value, scientifically speaking. Others might be useful, but science hasn't yet reached the point where it can recognize this value and make good use of it. Occasionally an accidental find, such as the discovery of penicillin, will come at a time when science is poised, as it were, awaiting just such a discovery. The find is accidental. The readiness for it is not. And indeed it might be said that because of this readiness, the find sooner or later, however accidental, was inevitable.

Because scientists are blessed with keen intelligence, they have been able to accomplish in a short space of time what nature, working through lower life forms, has required much, much longer to accomplish. Yet scientists, too, are a part of nature, and are working to achieve what are, for all their work, merely variations of natural phenomena.

Man is not a creature apart, as his vanity often leads him to think. It is unrealistic to say, as so many do, that man can "conquer" nature. He can only cooperate with nature, as all creatures have done, and thereby come at a few of her unnumbered secrets.

The difference between deliberately experimenting with heredity, and allowing heredity to take place with no thought for the outcome, is more apparent than actual. Whether a person keeps poodles with longer ears because he likes long-eared poodles, or because he deliberately intends to develop a new longer-eared breed, the effect will be the same. His droopy-eared pets, living and mating together, will eventually produce the new strain. The only difference will be that without deliberate breeding, the effect may require more time for its accomplishment, fewer restrictions being placed on the poodles' mating habits. But if the man lives long enough, and if he persists in his special liking for long-eared poodles, the end will be accomplished whether he looks for it or not. In both cases the creative factor is not the molding force of a sculptor's chisel, working to change a single block of stone into some other predetermined shape, but only a *present* interest in poodles with longer ears.

And the same will hold true for the evolving leopard. The leopard will not set out to organize spotted leopards into an SDBS (Society for the Development of Better Spots). But it will, if possible, be drawn to habitats where spots will prove more useful. In these habitats it will meet other spotted cats with similar ideas for "beating the system." With some of these it will mate, and so the strain, once started, will increase.

It is not necessary, however, to limit conscious selection to the use life makes of available, but random, mutational opportunities. It can be claimed with some justification that that life *creates* those opportunities, even as, by seizing them, it opens the way to fresh opportunities.

Scientists, as we have said, render even their

accidental discoveries almost inevitable by their pre-paredness to make just such discoveries. Each time science evolves to a new level of understanding, numerous facts of nature are discovered that are relevant to its new understanding. In many cases, it wasn't that the facts themselves had not been noted before. They may have been noted frequently; they had simply not been found applicable to the knowledge so far at hand.

In evolution, similarly, if spots had appeared by mutation in a species that didn't live near a jungle, or that had no inclination for jungle living, the spotted mutants would have had a hard go of it, and would finally have disappeared. Other mutations would have occurred as well, but advantage would have been taken of only those for which the species was ready. That some of these, at least, should have occurred was, in the course of time, inevitable. When they did occur, the moment had come for an awaited change. Another deliberate step was taken on the pathway of evolution.

Thus, certain fishes of Devonian times chose to live in shallow waters—perhaps to escape the larger fish, or perhaps because the vegetation or the warmth attracted them. When incipient legs appeared in some of these "landlubbers," the time was ripe for a further change. The previous interest of these fish in landed areas had prepared them; they could now take advantage of these leg-like appendages, which in the ocean deeps would only have proved inconvenient to them. A few of this avant-garde species chose to use their rudimentary limbs to come out of the water. Again, this new choice directed the evolution of better legs.

Whether the choice was forced, as sometimes it must have been, by a dwindling food supply, or whether it was directed by sheer predilection, the fact is that it *was* a choice. And by this choice, acting on and reacting to environment, diversity in evolution can be very reasonably explained.

If evolution really is related to intelligence, one would expect it to be more rapid in the more intelligent species—in species that are quicker to take advantage of natural opportunities. This does, in fact, seem to have been the case.

Simpson, after comparing the evolutional rates of various species, concludes: "There is thus good concrete evidence for the impression that some animals have evolved much faster than others. There is less complete but still sufficient evidence for the further generalization that the vertebrates have tended to evolve (structurally) faster than the invertebrates."*

Exceptions to this generalization—the opossum, for example, whose evolution over the past 80 million years has been slow compared to that of other vertebrates—are also seen to be comparatively unintelligent. Thus, Simpson continues: "There is a general impression that the 'higher' groups . . . have evolved more rapidly than the lower."[†]

This ratio of the speed of structural evolution to the level of intelligence should not be looked upon as an inflexible rule. Evolutional change, in terms of physical structure, is not a necessary consequence of intelligent

* Ibid., pp. 99, 100.

† Ibid., p. 100.

adaptation. Where an existing structure continues to serve an organism's changing needs, it is less probable that new structures will replace the old.

A naturalistic (as opposed to a supernaturalistic) view of intelligence shows the whole process of selection to have in it something of conscious purpose. Where purpose ends and randomness begins would be, indeed, impossible to say. But that purpose is nonexistent is an entirely untenable concept.

All one may say is that the purpose in evidence reveals no pushing and prodding on the part of some Heavenly Dictator. (And wouldn't an absolute divine destiny imply a more mechanical evolutionary process than that suggested by biologists? It would mean that living creatures were no more than pieces in a game, moved here and there at the sheer whim of the Mover.)

Nor does intelligent selection imply necessarily an *all wise* selection. (The staunchest proponent of an intelligent *elan vital* would never think of sitting down to a game of chess with a rhododendron bush.)

The fact is that discussions of the subject have taken people in circles. Biologists certainly would not deny the influence of intelligence, or at least of some conscious drive, on the process of natural selection. Intelligent choice is simply not their immediate concern; hence their willingness to push this aspect of the subject into the background, while they busy themselves with gene mutations, survival statistics, and other biological mechanisms.

Vitalists, again, will certainly not deny that mistakes play a part in evolution, however intelligent the process may be as a whole.

And not even the hardiest finalist would deny that *absolute* perfection cannot be found anywhere in this world, the basic constituent of which—matter—is so riddled with imperfections.

We have only to expand our horizons to discover a strong possibility that all three views are correct, each on its own level of application.

The issue of whether or not living organisms can direct their own evolution by deliberate mutation is not a crucial one. The organisms will seek situations, or will develop skills and interests within present situations, that will favor certain mutations, and inhibit others. Mutations, again, will direct new lines of development that will, in their turn, favor new mutations.

It will be an interactive process between the organism and its environment. On lower life levels, especially, it will be mostly a blind process. And yet, even here there will exist an inchoate but growing element of self-direction.

Even the planarian, a humble flatworm, can be trained to avoid undesirable situations (channels leading to an electric shock) and to seek desirable ones (channels leading to food). With such a capacity for choice, however rudimentary, at its disposal, who is to say that the planarian may not, occasionally, seek out or in other ways prepare itself for conditions that will favor the evolution of new life forms?

The worm need not actually think (and obviously doesn't think, any more than most people do, for that matter) of evolving new forms. It is sufficient that its own inclinations give it, occasionally, a new *direction.*

It is even sufficient if its present interests be broad enough, without new direction, for it to seize new opportunities when presented to it in mutational form.

"Where there's life, there's hope." At any rate, where there is life there is awareness of some sort, however dim. And this awareness, acting within the framework of natural law, cannot but exert an influence on an animal's behavior, an influence which must in time affect its evolutional development.

CHAPTER TEN

Meaning in Evolution?
Part II

WHAT IS LIFE?

What is life? Is it only a combination of chemicals, of atoms and molecules? Religionists and others who believe in a meaningful scheme of things usually reject out of hand any such notion. Unfortunately for their claims, their support rests entirely on untested assumptions and abstract intellectual arguments. All the actual evidence supports the conclusions of materialists:

Life is not separate from matter. It arises spontaneously when atomic molecules unite in the requisite combinations.

CHAPTER TEN

Meaning in Evolution?
Part II

WHAT IS LIFE?

"VERY WELL," says the materialist, "I don't mind admitting that consciousness may exert some influence on evolution. But I object strenuously to the idea that vitalism—what to speak of finalism!—may be as justifiable, in its own way, as materialism. The opposition is irreconcilable. Materialism can never admit the claim of vitalists that life and consciousness share no common ground with material principles. Every scientific finding supports the view that all things are bound by natural law, that life, consciousness—these, too, are one with material phenomena."

And so, we ask, your claim is that this oneness reduces them to the status of simple mechanisms?

"Most certainly," he replies. "For what is life? It is merely the result of a chance combination of chemicals! What is consciousness? It is the product of the movement of electrons in a pattern of nerve circuits. Poetic inspirations, the counsels of sages—all the 'lofty concepts' of man are nothing but the manipulation of memory traces in the brain. The very factor of choice that you present is purely a matter of mechanics. Whether intelligent leopard or intelligent scientist, it is all a question of cause and effect, of action and reaction—of mechanics!"

"Ah, no!" cries the vitalist, rushing anxiously onto the scene. "Life is a cause; it is not an effect. Its decisions spring from within itself. Its actions may be adaptive, but only to a degree. Essentially, they represent some agency that stands above material law, and that acts upon matter, but that is not acted upon by it. Life and matter can never be united under a single law!"

Will anything unravel this tangle? Certainly the materialist is not lacking in scientific support for his claim. But the vitalist, too, seems to be right. Life does act upon matter. It is not subject to the simple laws of cause and effect that operate on a material level. I push a chair, and it moves in the direction I have pushed it. I start to push a dog, and he may walk away, or try to bite me, before I can even touch him. Obviously, there is at least a difference in behavior. And, scientifically speaking, behavior is the only valid consideration.

But does this behavioral difference indicate a difference *in essence*? After all, not even matter behaves always in a simple "push-me-pull-you" manner. Its bag of tricks is fairly bulging, what with mysterious principles of magnetism, radioactivity, and other forms of subtle energy. The force of gravity can't be shoved about like a chair either, yet we don't summon this fact to demonstrate that gravity is therefore animate.

Consider, then: If matter under certain conditions can become radioactive, why might it not, under certain other conditions, produce life? Why plead a difference merely on the basis of behavior?

A fascinating piece of information has come out in recent years. Biochemists have broken living organisms down to their irreducible essential: nucleic acid, as DNA and RNA molecules. Even at this basic level, be it noted, no sign has emerged of anything operating independently of natural law.

In 1958, V.G. Allfrey and A.E. Mirsky reported that they had isolated cell nuclei and had removed therefrom the nucleic acid. The well-known biochemist and scientific writer, Isaac Asimov, describes their findings:

> At once the ability of the nucleus to manufacture protein came to an end. If the nucleic acid were replaced, the ability to manufacture protein was restored. What was particularly startling, however, was that if, instead of nucleic acid, a synthetic polymer (resembling the nucleic acid only in having a long-chain molecule with similar distribution of electric charge) were added to the nucleus, protein manufacture was restored.*

It is astonishing indeed to find that a synthetic substance can give living cells the power to carry on their essential life processes.

But the Nobel Prize–winning chemist, Wendell M. Stanley, has made an even more astonishing statement.

---

* Isaac Asimov, *The Wellsprings of Life* (Abelard-Schuman, Ltd., New York, 1969), p. 201.

"There is the more distant possibility," he writes, "of creating at least a very simple living organism from scratch, from laboratory chemicals."*

How did this amazing thing called life get started in the first place? Who could say, categorically? But there is considerable evidence that it came about quite naturally. Laboratory experiments have proved that when fast-moving particles such as cosmic rays strike the atmosphere, they can produce formaldehyde and other organic compounds. Lightning has been found to produce amino acids. The same effect has been achieved artificially by ultraviolet rays.[†] Asimov reports:

> In 1952, an American chemist, S.L. Miller, circulated a mixture of water, ammonia, methane and hydrogen past an electrical discharge for a week, trying to duplicate primordial conditions (with the electric discharge representing the energy supply of ultraviolet light). At the end of the week, he found organic compounds in his solution that had not been there to begin with. Even some of the simpler amino acids were present—and he had been working only a week.[‡]

In 1946 Wendell M. Stanley won the Nobel Prize in chemistry for his success in isolating, purifying, and crystallizing a living virus, thereby providing convincing evidence that viruses have a dual nature: Under certain

---

* Wendell M. Stanley and Evans G. Valens, *Viruses and the Nature of Life* (E.P. Dutton & Co., Inc., New York), p. 10.

† Scientists believe that in the early stages of our planet's history, the ultraviolet rays from the sun were much stronger than they are now; they reached the earth's surface unhindered by the cushion of oxygen which now protects it.

‡ Op. cit., p. 33.

conditions they are simply lifeless crystals, like sugar or table salt. But under others, they spring to life, reproduce, mutate, and—as everyone knows—cause diseases in plants and animals.

Writes Stanley: "The qualities which distinguish the living from the non-living are not so obvious after all."*

Indeed, the sometime lifelessness of life on other levels of manifestation is a frequent source of astonishment.

Consider the case of the Tardigrada, microscopic arthropods that, to quote the geologist J.H.F. Umbgrove, "can remain in a dried up condition of latent animation for ten or more years, and then, when placed in water, swell out again and go on living quite happily."†

There is further evidence to support the possibility—unthinkable to vitalists—that even in basic matters of behavior there is more similarity between animate and inanimate matter than is generally supposed.

Karl Friedrich Bohhoeffer, Germany's foremost physical chemist and, from 1949–1957, head of the prestigious Max Planck Institute for Physical Chemistry in Göttingen, devoted the last sixteen years of his life to experiments dealing "with membrane potentials and with the activation of passive iron as a physico-chemical model of nerve excitation."‡ Of the latter experiments, Bonhoeffer wrote:

* Op. cit., p. 204.

† J.H.F. Umbgrove, *Symphony of the Earth* (Martinus Nijhoff, The Hague, Holland, 1950), p. 199.

‡ *Nature,* July 6, 1957.

It is indeed most astonishing that iron wire and nerve, which from the chemical point of view differ so enormously, function in such a similar way. It does not seem credible that the various functional properties in which the two systems resemble each other could be independent and accidental similarities. There is here a most interesting problem from the point of view of reaction kinetics. The existence of a threshold of activation, of a tendency to give rhythmic reactions, and a suggestion that even the so-called accommodation effects are not missing in the model, indicated that all these properties, so uncommon in ordinary chemistry, are in some way related to one another.*

Other scientists have made similar discoveries, among them Wilhelm Ostwald, Heathcote, and Lillie. One of the pioneers in this field of inquiry was the great Indian scientist, Sir Jagadis Chandra Bose. In the early years of this century, Bose conducted a series of experiments on response in the living and the nonliving. After testing response to electrical and chemical stimuli in nerve tissue, in plants, and in inorganic substances, he came to a number of astonishing conclusions.

"The diphasic variations as exhibited by metals," he wrote of one experiment, "are in every way counterparts of similar phenomena observed in animal tissues."

Countless physical functions, usually considered peculiar to living organisms, were found by Bose to have their exact counterparts in inorganic matter. Take for example the matter of vision. Bose noted:

---

* Reprinted in translation in *The Journal of General Physiology,* Vol. 32, The Rockefeller Institute for Medical Research, New York, 1949, from *Zeitschrift für Physikalische Chemie.*

The response of the sensitive [liquid] inorganic cell, to the stimulus of light, is in every way similar to that of the retina. In both we have, under normal conditions, a positive variation; in both the intensity of response up to a certain limit increases with the duration of illumination; it is affected, in both alike, by temperature; in both there is comparatively little fatigue; the increase of response with intensity of stimulus is similar in both; and finally, even in abnormalities—such as reversal of response, preliminary negative twitch on commencement, and terminal positive twitch on cessation of illumination, and decline and reversal under continued action of light—parallel effects are noticed . . . There is not a single phenomenon in the responses, normal or abnormal, exhibited by the retina, which has not its counterpart in the sensitive cell constructed of inorganic material.*

Bose concluded: "The response phenomena are exhibited not only by plants but by inorganic substances as well, and the responses are modified by various conditions in exactly the same manner as those of animal tissues."

By contrast with the similarities of inanimate matter to living organisms, Dr. Frank A. Brown, Jr., Morrison Professor of Biology at Northwestern University, discovered that organic life will respond to certain stimuli that are generally supposed to affect only metals. Dr. Brown wanted to see whether the earth's magnetic field might also affect living organisms. His conclusion, based on exhaustive experiments:

There remains no reasonable doubt that living systems are extraordinarily sensitive to magnetic fields. By

---

* Sir J.C. Bose, *Response in the Living and the Non-Living* (Longmans, Green, & Co., London, 1902).

extremely simple experiments it is possible to prove that highly diverse types of animals and plants may have their orientation modified by artificial fields [created by bar magnets] of the order of strength of the geomagnetic field.*

Bose concluded his own observations with the statement: "The investigations which have just been described may possibly carry us one step further, proving to us that these things are determined, not by the play of an unknown and arbitrary vital force, but by the working of laws that know no change, acting equally and uniformly throughout the organic and the inorganic worlds."†

Indeed, by one path or another the conclusion seems inescapable. The hope of vitalists to prove a fundamental difference between matter and life seems doomed to disappointment. It is almost certain that animate and inanimate matter are but different aspects of a single reality.

And finalists may howl, but it remains undeniably correct to speak, as Bose does elsewhere, of the life processes as "physico-chemical phenomena." For if all phenomena are related, it is perfectly proper to interpret them in terms of one another. Since steam is nothing but vaporized water, one may speak of it in terms of water, even though its present appearance is so different from that of water.

Life, then, is not something new that has been intro-

---

* F.H. Barnwell and F.A. Brown, Jr., *Biological Effects of Magnetic Fields* (Plenum Press, New York, 1964).

† Op. cit.

duced from outside into the material universe. It has its origins deep in the sands of inanimate matter.

CHAPTER ELEVEN

Meaning in Evolution?
Part III

WHAT IS MATTER?

Life, materialistic thinkers tell us, is only an expression of inanimate matter. Does this mean that life itself is essentially inanimate?

It would make better sense, surely, to say that "inanimate" matter has been shown to be a great deal more living *than men have hitherto supposed, possessing as it does the marvelous capacity to manifest life.*

CHAPTER ELEVEN

Meaning in Evolution?
Part III

WHAT IS MATTER?

IF IT IS TRUE THAT LIFE ORIGINATES in inanimate matter, then what *is* matter, that it can give rise to life?

For it must be clear that the *appearance* of life cannot signify its creation out of nothing. The bar of metal that becomes magnetized doesn't *create* magnetism; it merely acquires it, or manifests a quality that was already latent within it. The atom that is split doesn't create energy; it merely releases it. How, then, may matter be said to *create* life? Obviously, all that it can do is *manifest* life.

If all phenomena are related, it is perfectly feasible to interpret them in terms of one another. If steam is vaporized water, then water, by the same token, is condensed steam. If life and matter really are aspects of one reality, then matter must be quite as living as life itself is material. To shrug off life as *merely* material would be to ignore the visible evidence of the vast potentials this supposedly "inert" matter keeps locked in its heart.

"Well, all right," one may concede, "so life is not *merely* material; matter is not *merely* inert. But these admissions don't force us to abandon a materialistic stand. All we need do is think of life as some sort of organized energy—yes, *merely* energy!"

True, this does seem possible—even from a non-materialistic standpoint. It is interesting that in India the word for life and for energy is the same: *prana.* After all, why not? In common parlance, when we say, "I feel wonderfully *alive* today!" we mean simply that we feel unusually energetic. When a person, after a long illness, or a period of depression, tells us that he has "come back to life," it is his normal energy level, not his existence, that has been restored. It seems logical enough, certainly, to see life itself in terms of organized energy.

But of *merely* energy? Come now, let us omit this word, "merely." For energy, too, must be as exalted by its equation with life as matter is.

Consider what endless versatility life—whether as matter or as energy—has assumed! The plumed birds soaring in shafts of sunlight, proud of their beauty; the beavers, born engineers, constructing mighty dams; the bees bobbing patterns in their hives, informing their companions by complex signals where the flowers grow; the midges dancing in perfect unison on strings of summer air; and man, insatiably inventive, forming endless cloud-fancies into solid shapes—"To what end?" one might ask, yet how wonderful all the same!

Consider above all the greatest wonder: consciousness,

this marvelous mystery, as close to me as myself, as far from me as my farthest dreams, the one phenomenon whose reality I cannot possibly question without, by the very questioning, demonstrating its existence. Life may be a sort of organized energy, but in that case it is energy, certainly, in no blind, mechanistic sense.

What *is* consciousness? How did it first appear on the scene? How did intelligence evolve? Our materialist claims that thinking is "merely" (again that word!) a "manipulation of memory traces in the brain." Granted; why not? But is that the whole story? *Is thinking the same thing as consciousness?* One cannot but ask: Who is the operator? Who does the manipulating?

Some people argue that when thoughts cease—as, for example, in deep sleep—one loses consciousness. But if this be true, why is it that one usually knows, on awaking, how well he has slept? Why, again, becoming uncomfortable in his sleep, does he shift his position? Or, if too warm, does he—even without waking up—throw off the offending blankets? And how does he know when he is sufficiently rested to return to wakefulness?

Indeed, it is well known these days that our so-called "conscious" mind represents only the surface of our consciousness. An ocean of awareness heaves silently within us. Conflicting tides of desires, emotions, and impulses, of which we may be superficially unaware, may yet keep us in a state of tension and turmoil. It is a mistake (however, one that is often committed) to speak of this vast subconscious realm as the "unconscious." The tumult of incoming sensations may *seem* to dismiss subtler motives and feelings, but these lurk quietly in the back of our minds nonetheless, and it is our consciousness alone that gives them reality.

Thought is an *act* of consciousness. To say, to the contrary, that thinking creates consciousness is as careless an explanation as it would be to say that splitting the atom *creates* energy, or that matter in certain combinations *creates* life. Is it not self-evident that it takes awareness to think? Sight would be impossible without the power to see. How could thoughts occur without the power—that is to say, the consciousness—to think them?

"Programmed" the brain may be indeed, as scientists say that it is. Thinking may well be a "manipulation of memory traces in the brain." But the whole process smacks of something far from automatic. Some sort of censorship exists, obviously. Two people in the same environment will observe it differently, and will observe different things in it. Identical twins, raised from infancy in different environments, have been found to be more alike in their interests than fraternal twins raised in the same homes.*

Environmental programming, evidently, is only a part of the story. Someone there is who picks and chooses, from incoming information, that which will be meaningful particularly to him.

What, then, if our thinking processes do have their mechanical aspects? The brain has to function *somehow.*

* Ref. *Science Digest,* December 1964, "Heredity vs. Environment—a Surprising New Answer," by Dr. and Mrs. Jules Kaplan. Based on research conducted with forty-four sets of monozygotic twins (identical, from the same egg) who had been raised separately from infancy, this article reported: "Identical twins who had seldom or never met before tested much more alike in personality, intelligence, attitudes and mannerisms than fraternal twins from separate eggs brought up in the same house."

Life needs a body for physical manifestation, and the body must obey mechanical principles to function at all in this world. Why should it be otherwise with the mind?

But who is the operator, say? Who does the manipulating? Surely someone, or something, seems to be at the controls. "*I am,* therefore I think," would be a truer dictum than Descartes's, "I think, therefore I am."

No one knows to what extent conscious intelligence may be developed. Conversely, no one knows from what pristine beginnings it has sprung. The smallest organisms act as if moved by a purpose—deliberate, however limited, and however blind and unreasoning. As George Gaylord Simpson pointed out: "I know that many students of the subject deny that any animals below man, or certainly the really lowly types, are 'aware' or 'perceive' anything whatsoever . . . [yet] all animals *act* as if they had awareness and perception—even the amoeba does." *

And Dr. Kenneth Walker, in his book, *Diagnosis of Man,* testified:

> As a surgeon, I am sometimes called upon to cut away the ureter (the narrow channel that connects the bladder with the kidney) and to implant it into another part of the bladder. When my work has been completed I am ashamed of its crudity. Compared with the job done by a plumber, my joint is a poor and botched concern. Yet when I examine it a year after I am scarcely able to tell which is Nature's joint and which is my own. Some intelligence in the patient's body has made good my failure, paring off redundant tissue here, adding new tissue there, until perfection has been attained. Does that intelligence exist only in the brain? No, for if I divide all the nerves

* George Gaylord Simpson, op. cit., p. 258f.

that reach that spot from the brain, the work is performed just as well.*

Consciousness does clearly seem to exist on levels far lower than any we would consider intelligent. To judge from behavior, at least, the appearance of consciousness would seem to be coincidental with that of life. And even there the story does not appear to end. For is existence confined to physical appearances? Not at all. Life doesn't appear out of nothing. How can consciousness do so?

As Bergson put it: "It appears extremely likely that consciousness, originally immanent in all that lives, is dormant where there is no longer spontaneous movement, and awakens when life tends to free activity." Were one to trace the process backward toward its origins, one would encounter only dimmer and dimmer states of awareness, but never, presumably, total unawareness—even as an object might be shrunk indefinitely without ever becoming nothing.

We have accustomed ourselves to thinking in linear terms. In a straight line, whatever moves goes *from* something *to* something else; so long as it continues to progress, it can never return to any point that has been left behind. In modern science, however, space itself is generally conceived of as spherical. In whatever direction one proceeds,

---

* Dr. Kenneth Walker, *Diagnosis of Man* (Jonathan Cape, London, 1948), p. 104. Dr. Walker speaks here of an "intelligence." But his use of this word is obviously not in the usual sense of the rational faculty. It must be noted that this "intelligence" requires a year to complete its job, in contrast to the doctor's work of a few minutes. No unflattering comparison need be assumed here to man's intelligence, however short of final perfection the doctor's share of the work.

one ends up at last where he began. Say, rather, on a sphere there can be no question of any beginning or ending.

Philosophically speaking, this modern concept illustrates the teaching that nothing can be brought into manifestation that does not exist in some form already. In the words of the Indian scripture: "That which is not shall never be; that which is, shall never cease to be."*

Consciousness, as a simple fact or condition of awareness, is not bound to *express* itself at all in order to exist. Existence precedes expression. Indeed, consciousness may well be found to be latent in all matter—or, like certain forms of energy, to exist even where matter does not exist.

The coexistence of matter and consciousness is a fact in any case. And it raises an interesting problem: How is it possible to *equate* two such apparent opposites? They must be aspects of the same reality, but how so? What *is* that reality?

Let us approach this problem in self-contradiction by first considering a more common equation: matter and energy. How can solid matter be one and the same thing as energy, even to say nothing of consciousness? The answer is: because matter isn't really solid; essentially, it *is* energy.

The converse, however, is not true: Energy is not composed of ultra-fine particles of solid matter.

It is at least exceedingly probable, therefore, that of the two, energy is the more basic, and the primal "substance" from which matter is derived.

Matter, then, though real enough on its own level of

* The Bhagavad Gita, II:16.

reality, would seem to be real in the last analysis only as a manifestation of subtler realities. Matter manifests life, true, but more basically still (if life and energy have anything in common) it would rather seem that life manifests matter.

Certain physical combinations make possible the physical manifestations of life, as the surface of a pond gives visible evidence of the unseen movements of the wind. Yet from our present standpoint, matter is itself that life, even as the rippling water is actually composed of the very gases (hydrogen and oxygen) that blow upon it with the wind.

This argument becomes irresistible when we consider consciousness. For matter can be equated with consciousness only if matter *is* essentially conscious. It would be unconscionable to say that consciousness is essentially unconscious. *If matter can manifest consciousness, it can only be because the essential substance of matter IS consciousness.*

A number of eminent scientists have suggested that consciousness might well be the essential substance of matter. Writing of the implications inherent in a nonmechanical universe, Sir James Jeans remarked:

> The old dualism of mind and matter . . . seems likely to disappear, not through matter becoming in any way more shadowy or insubstantial than heretofore, or through mind becoming resolved into a function of the working of matter, but through substantial matter resolving itself into a creation and manifestation of mind.*

* James Jeans, *The Mysterious Universe* (E.P. Dutton & Co., Inc., New York, 1958), p. 181.

And in the same vein, Sir Arthur Eddington wrote:

> The recent discoveries of science do, I believe, take us to an eminence from which we can look down into the deep waters of philosophy; and if I rashly plunge into them, it is not because I have confidence in my powers of swimming, but to try to show that the water is really deep. To put the conclusion crudely—the stuff of the world is mind-stuff.*

When one thinks of it, to insist on a mechanistic interpretation of everything as the only valid one—to say, for instance, that living persons are only machines, because their bodies and brains function in a somewhat mechanical fashion—is even stranger than the contrary superstition of savages, who ascribe a living personality to every stone. *We know,* after all, that we are alive, that we are aware. Ultimately speaking, we can judge the world only in terms of our awareness. To imagine that rocks have man-like personalities is a very natural mistake. But to try to convince ourselves that *we* take after the rocks in their essential lifelessness and unawareness—this is a completely unnatural presumption. The joke of it is that it requires an act of most unrock-like intellection to make such a presumption at all.

It really looks as though, in our Western approach to reality, we have been selling consciousness short. It is perfectly all right to speak of mechanisms, and of statistics of motion and measurement, but it is foolish to become so hypnotized by statistics that one imagines them, rather than the entities they describe, to be the reality.

---

* Sir Arthur Eddington, *The Nature of the Physical World* (Ann Arbor Paperbacks, University of Michigan, 1958), p. 276.

Statistics are merely symbols—convenient rational categories that make possible certain levels of thought. As with all categorical thinking, however, it is easy to reach a point of imagining that the objects described are symbols of their statistics, rather than the reverse.

Thus, a horse that can run twenty-five miles an hour might be considered a symbol of speed—a reasonable idea, too, if abstract speed alone is being considered. But the horse does many other things besides run. And even the totality of what it does would not tell the whole story of what it *is*—and, because of what it is, what it might do in novel situations.

It is all very well to see life in terms of mechanistic principles. It is very reasonable to point out the underlying similarity of all things, living and inert. But when an effort is made to explain all things *wholly* in terms of inert mechanisms, the defects of this categorical approach become glaringly obvious.

It would be impossible for a stupid person to imitate the subtle physical signs of a keen intelligence: the bright, alert eyes, the firm smile, the instinctively affirmative gestures of hand and head—to name but a few of the common signs. Similarly, one cannot but wonder how, if the universe has no intelligence behind it, it has managed to manifest so many signs of a mighty intelligence.

"Only God can make a tree." Evidently He didn't actually *make* it, personally and specially, the way a carpenter makes a table. Nor is the tree itself some sort of genius that can, by reason of its cleverness, do things that no man has been able to duplicate. Some sort of intelligence certainly seems to be at work, however, a sort of general consciousness of which we, too, are a partial expression.

Lower forms of life, being less aware, require more time to work out their problems, and solve these to varying degrees of perfection or imperfection. Whatever the speed, however, the signs are there, and we ourselves demonstrate, at least subconsciously, our recognition of the fact by giving the work of duplicating nature's processes to brilliant scientists.

Indeed, if there be no intelligence in Nature, why is it that we human beings, with all *our* intelligence, keep looking to Nature to find out how we ought to do things?

Who but a blind or completely insensitive person could write off the wonders of the universe as purely "meaningless" and "accidental"? Whether it all required billions of years to take place, or the imaginary six days of Genesis—what essential difference, really, *in eternity,* where time is not a factor at all? That life and evolution happened, that they were *bound* to happen somehow, somewhere—this, and not how long it took, is the crucial point.

How marvelous, indeed, is even the simple fact of milk from a mother's breast.

How marvelous, the way a redwood tree compensates for the loss of some of its roots. Consider for a moment this little natural miracle. As, with the loss of those roots, the tree begins to lean, it seeks new support by building a buttress. This it does by changing its ring pattern. On the buttress side, much wider rings begin to appear; on the opposite side, the newly formed rings are very fine. The wood in the buttress is of a different type from that normal to a redwood tree; it is known as "compression" wood. To consider this elaborate process to be *only* a matter of mechanics requires an act of faith, truly— perhaps as great as any called for in the churches!

Consider a simple, but vital, natural problem: How is a newborn baby protected from bleeding to death when the umbilical cord is cut? In the cord there is a special jelly, which expands as soon as the cord is exposed to air; the flow of blood in the cord is automatically cut off. Is it possible that no purpose at all lies behind this vital process?

How marvelous, indeed, are the provisions life makes for countless phases of its development!

It is even possible that scientists will someday discover that consciousness *is,* after all, one of the influencing factors in gene mutation. Nowadays this possibility is generally ridiculed. But not by all scientists. Sir Arthur Thomson, the famous scientific writer, stated:

There can be no return to the old belief in the transmission of any and every individually acquired character, but it is probable that we shall discover by and by that individual experiences count for something in evolution.*

And why not? It has been proved that thoughts can affect the chemistry of the body. Why not—if only to some extent, and occasionally—the chemistry of the genes?

---

* Sir J. Arthur Thomson, *Riddles of Science,* revised by Bernard Jaffe (Premier Books, New York, 1961), paperback, p. 217.

How else to account for the strangely complex phenomenon of instinct in the insects? Certainly it does look as if experience at some point in evolution gave rise to the complex behavior patterns that an insect follows instinctively, often with no opportunity to learn them from any of its living fellows.

The wasp egg, for example, is buried by the mother in an underground passage, with a paralyzed caterpillar for the grub to feed on when it emerges from the egg. The mother dies before her offspring are hatched. She never sees the result of her handiwork. Her offspring, in their turn, never learn how they should handle their eggs. How do successive mother wasps know what they must do to continue their line?

How, again, by mechanical genetics alone, can one account for another riddle—this one an apparent contradiction of the law of Mendelian inheritance? It is a truism, observable in every country, that people of spiritual, sensitive, or highly creative natures generally live less on the sex plane than people of gross physical inclinations. This is not a question of custom, evidently, but simply of the way man is made: Energy cannot be channeled in either direction, whether higher or lower, without diverting it at least to some extent from the other.

Indeed, many of the world's greatest geniuses have never married at all; their work has completely absorbed their time and energies.*

The probability of more offspring being born to

---

* Among great Westerners numerous names spring to mind: Beethoven, Brahms, Leonardo da Vinci, Michelangelo, Newton, Galileo, Pascal, Kant, Schopenhauer, Nietzsche—to name but a handful of many.

people of strong sensual appetites is, quite obviously, considerable. Yet the sensitivity and creativeness of the human race cannot honestly be said to be on the decline. Many of the greatest strides of civilization have been taken only in recent decades.

One may well wonder, indeed, how the higher tendencies in man ever got off to a fair biological start. According to Mendelian inheritance, at least, boorishness and stupidity should be on the increase. But evidently they are not.

Numerous question marks hang over the entire picture. One thing, however, seems almost certain: The biological sciences, once they have consolidated their information on life's mechanisms, will begin to find themselves forced to veer toward a less mechanistic view.

If physics has had to expand its views from pure mechanisms to increasingly subtle energies, then biology, surely, will come in time to expand its own views from mechanics to consciousness—consciousness, not as a foreign imposition on physical realities, but as a part, with them, of some greater reality.

CHAPTER TWELVE

Meaning in Evolution?
Part IV

IS EVOLUTION PROGRESSIVE?

*Is evolution progressive? Orthodox biologists say that
it is not. Indeed, considering the criteria they propose,
progress of any kind isn't really an issue. Any apparent "up" might just as easily be due to a relative
"down" somewhere else.*

*Science does, however, discern one movement that
is universal: the expansion of the entire universe in
relation to itself. In this fact we establish a basis for a
new view of natural selection, one in which progress—
and sometimes its opposite, regress—can be observed
in the entire evolutional scheme.*

CHAPTER TWELVE

Meaning in Evolution?
Part IV

IS EVOLUTION PROGRESSIVE?

*Nobody can foresee whether these modern specu-
lations (on the problems of life and matter) will
ever be susceptible to condensation into a social
or religious system. Remarkably enough, however, they remind one of certain aspects of the
Brahmanese Upanishads.*
—J.H.F. Umbgrove, in *Symphony of the Earth*

WE ARE CLOSING IN on an important question: Is evolution
progressive? Is it meaningful? Or is it merely multifarious?

Biologists of course repudiate the idea of progress.
How could they support such a notion when to them
anything that happens does so accidentally? This meaningless outlook was perhaps best stated by James F. Crow
in an article in *Scientific American* (the September, 1959,
issue). Rhetorically, Crow asked, "Has man changed
more in developing his brain than the elephant has by
growing a trunk?"

To the layman this question will appear absurd. Not so to the orthodox biologist; his answer would be, in effect, "We have no reason to say that man has changed more." As Simpson expressed it, "Evolution is not invariably accompanied by progress, nor does it really seem to be characterized by progress as an essential feature."*

The clue to this line of reasoning lies in the care scientists take not to impose their human values on the universe. Such caution is necessary. It should, however, be exercised as conscientiously in the other direction as well. For it is a mistake to be categorical in the claim, as so many have been, that the universe is utterly lacking in values. How do they know? There is no more justification for such a claim than for the insistence of medieval thinkers that the whole universe was subservient to their system of dogmas.

How much, really, is known about the subtler workings of matter? It might even turn out that certain human values do have their counterparts elsewhere in nature. We've seen good reason to claim that man is an integral part of nature—that his intelligence in no way separates him, except in degree, from other natural phenomena. His sense of values, then, too, must be considered a natural phenomenon.

Biologists have been too preoccupied with the simple statistics of survival. Granted, survival *is* the basic statistical factor in the evolutionary mechanism. In horse racing, the interest of the bettors is in how fast

* *The Meaning of Evolution,* p. 261.

the horses will run. In the race for survival, similarly—when that is how it is studied, as a race—all that matters is who wins. Progress, here, won't be a serious consideration, except in the more or less meaningless sense that species, in their struggle for existence, may grow larger, or fleeter, or spottier, or more intelligent.

There is nothing progressive about the bare fact of survival. However big or intelligent a species becomes, if managing not to die off is all that matters, one must admit that these changes, in themselves, are irrelevant. The simple fact of existence is no more real for a man than for an amoeba.

Even if one's view of survival is enlarged to include *talent* for survival as a criterion of progress, the oyster must be admitted to be as talented, in its own milieu, as man is in his. It is all a question of where you live, and of what challenges you have to meet. If man were suddenly compelled to live under water, he would be no match at all, evolutionally, for the oyster.

The difficulty lies in the fact that this universe is so infinitely unfixed. Small wonder that so many people consider it pointless! Literally speaking, that is just what it is; there are no fixed points of reference anywhere. All things must somehow plod their way over the shifting sands of relativity. A step forward may move the sand in such a way that one's actual motion is backward. In an absolute sense, indeed, one's direction of movement cannot be determined at all. It's a case of really not knowing whether one is coming or going.

From a standpoint of life's capacity for survival, one couldn't say definitely whether the dominance of a species was due to some inner vitality of its own (which would be an indication of progress), or because some rival species had begun to lose its vitality (which might suggest an overall decline). In relativity, motion cannot be said to be absolute.

Universally speaking, however, there *is* one sort of "absolute" motion—if the universe as a whole is taken *in relation to itself.*

To say that the universe is moving in one direction or another would be impossible. Scientists are agreed, however, that, *in relation to itself, the universe is expanding.* The speed of this movement cannot be determined absolutely, but *the direction of movement,* at least, has been ascertained *as an omnidirectional radiation outwards.*

And the same holds true for any system. Whether in relation to other objects it is moving forwards or backwards or left or right cannot be determined absolutely. But whether it is expanding or contracting *in relation to itself*—this, in spite of all other relationships, can be established definitely, not as a change in size (which would be a relative consideration), but as a radiation from within outward, or from without inward.

Preoccupation with survival has led biologists to think of nothing but objective developments—whether a tooth grows larger, or a claw sharper, or a trunk longer. From this standpoint, meaningfulness could not ever be established. From a standpoint of species themselves, however, of organisms themselves, it may be that a meaningful development can in fact be traced.

From this point of view it is, after all, meaningful that life has continuously expanded (to quote Simpson) "to fill in all the available space in the livable environments."* It indicates an expansive vitality in life itself, an experimental zest that cannot in any way be dismissed as "merely relative."

Ah, one may ask, but is this a valid expansion in a sense meaningful to us as human beings, with our inclination for moral values? Here we come to the crux of the matter.

For in this context, too, systems must be seen in relation to themselves. The question to be asked is: Has their development been in any way meaningful *to the organisms themselves?*

"Anthropomorphism!" Now the charge becomes inevitable. Scientific objectivity, however, can sometimes reach a point of evanescing returns. Certainly, one must be impartial in any search for understanding, and not project his personal inclinations onto subjects where those inclinations are not an issue. To make the *a priori* assumption, however, that he alone, or even mankind alone, can have any personal inclinations at all would be carrying objectivity too far.

Granted, it would be a mistake to imagine that, if you and I happen to like ice cream, everyone in the world must like it just as well. But if we say that just because we like ice cream, or anything else for that matter, our liking is no guarantee that others like anything at all, our "objectivity" will have been carried to self-defeating extremes.

Certain levels of self-understanding do make possible the only insights we ever receive into other people.

* Ibid., p. 243.

It is by our liking for ice cream that we can appreciate what motivates them when they struggle to acquire other things, even when their likes or dislikes differ widely from our own.

It seems reasonable to suppose that the same holds true for life generally. The fact that you and I like to walk gives us no good reason to assume that the snails grumble at being legless, but it may help us to appreciate something of their need for movement. There are levels, in other words, on which we and they, and probably all other creatures, share a common bond.

Life, for example, and the wish to perpetuate one's own life.

One of the basic facts of existence is the struggle for survival. Living organisms are engaged in a ceaseless battle to eat and to keep from being eaten. Why? *Why* this consummate eagerness to remain alive? Is it only mechanistic—a sort of inertia that, having once been set into motion, must continue until it is brought forcibly to a standstill? Yet even if such be the case, what we find here is no merely mechanical operation of Newton's law, but illustrates, rather, a link between physical mechanics and some higher principle. For, obviously, there is some sort of will in the organism itself to perpetuate its existence.

The question again: Why?

Surely the reason is, quite simply, that the animal's existence is, in some way, meaningful or worthwhile to itself. We use these words "meaningful" and "worthwhile" loosely, for lack of better expressions. But if there is a struggle for survival, it can only be to perpetuate existence *as a conscious experience,* and not as a mindless fact.

Conscious experience, then, not survival, is the key to progressive evolution. Survival alone would merely preserve the status quo; it is a static consideration. The will to experience, however, is expansive; it denotes a purposive urge, however vague or undirected. Animals do not rest satisfied with the mere continuation of their experience of life, by surviving; it seems clear that they also do their best to broaden that experience.

That the will to experience is an active force at every level of life may be seen from the fact that living organisms do so much more than struggle to survive.

Why does a monkey take a bite out of one fruit, then throw the perfectly good remainder away and reach for another fruit? Merely to survive? The first fruit would have suited its survival needs perfectly well. The only explanation that makes sense is that the monkey wanted the *experience* of tasting something else.

Why did an ancient fish with rudimentary legs make sallies onto the shore? Only because its legless relatives wouldn't let it eat in the water "with respectable folks"? More likely, the adventurous fish was impelled by a degree of curiosity—dim, perhaps, but actual. It could eat where it normally lived, but wanted to find out what the food tasted like somewhere else. For if sufficient food for survival were the only goal of a fish's existence, many an otherwise energetic fish need hardly move at all.

Why, in far-off times, did a primitive land animal with rudimentary wings try to use those appendages for flight? Only to escape some predator, or perhaps to get at food that it couldn't reach otherwise? Possibly. Yet very possibly, also, judging from the behavior we see in life all around us, it *enjoyed* the sensation of letting the wind lift a little of the weight off its legs. In breeding, it would have been inclined to mate with others of similarly buoyant spirits. Thus, one presumes, a process of natural selection was begun that resulted, finally, in the bird kingdom.

And why does a chicken cross the road? Ask any child that riddle and you'll get your answer: "Because it wants to get to the other side!"

Watching animals in their natural habitat, it is obvious that a great many of their movements are directed by their sheer delight at being able to leap, jump, fly, and even tease one another.

And here's another evolutional puzzle: How to explain, except in terms of a desire for greater awareness, the paradox of the size of man's brain?

This question has long been a puzzle to biologists. From a standpoint of competition and survival alone, a very slight increase in intelligence over that of other animals would be quite enough to keep mankind alive and prowling the plains. Man's brain, however, relative to his body's size, is about three times as large as that of the next most intelligent land animal. Why?

Surely it is man's desire for experience, and not merely for survival, that sets him so radically apart in this important respect.

Simpson himself points out that the struggle for survival is by no means the only factor active in evolution.

The process, according to Simpson, is rather one of progressive adaptation to environment, in which the struggle for survival plays only one role, albeit an important one.

But the question is not even merely one of adaptation. Water will mold itself submissively to the contours of its basin. Living organisms are not so acquiescent. An animal would crawl out of its basin, food or no food, comfort or no comfort, to see what lies on the other side of that nearby hill.

Clearly, evolution does represent more than change. In terms of life's own deepest and most instinctive drive there is a trend toward ever more expansive, more dynamic awareness.

The fishlike creature with stubby legs that comes out onto dry land not only begins a new evolutional trend toward lungs and legs; it also places a certain premium on curiosity. Its curiosity, moreover, and that of its fellow adventurers with whom it mixes, tends to evolve a species in which curiosity, and a capacity for the satisfaction of that curiosity, will be just a little bit more pronounced.

The newly spotted leopard, by using its spots to the best advantage, is not only learning to be crafty, personally. It is also directing evolution towards greater cunning, and eventually towards greater intelligence. The successful leopards, evolutionally speaking, will be those making the most *creative* use of their natural spotty endowment.

In the simpler life forms, as the abilities to see, hear, and feel are developed, an evolutional premium is placed, again, on awareness.

It seems safe to say that, in the lower animals, this trend expresses itself only vaguely beyond the simple desire to continue living. Evolution at those levels is less clearly motivated, because life at those levels is still so imperfectly aware. In the higher animals, however, motivation becomes clarified as a desire, not merely for a continuation of life, but for an expansion of awareness, and, in the expansion, for the *enjoyment* of life.

In mankind, evolution no longer requires new life forms through which to continue life's expansive urge. For man in his present form is capable of a vast expansion of awareness: from almost animalistic dullness to the highest levels of genius—indeed, to the highest spiritual attainments, such as those of a Buddha or a Jesus Christ.

The more expanded the awareness of a human being, the more he comes to see enjoyment as an abstraction, and not limited, therefore, to things or to specific experiences: as something, rather, that can be pursued for its own sake.

Man at the lowest level of human evolution—a person, that is to say, whose awareness is dim, and confined to his own self-interest—equates fulfillment with sensual pleasures. At higher levels of human evolution, however, with the appearance of a keener and more expanded awareness, there arises naturally in human nature a subtler understanding of fulfillment: less sensual, and more mental and spiritual.

Abstract thoughts, at higher levels of human evolution, can be intensely satisfying, as can inspiration and intangible feelings such as peace, happiness, and selfless love. Lofty sentiments are appreciated as far more enjoyable than a good meal. Expansive insights into the nature of reality, high ideals, and spiritual faith become things for which refined human beings would give up any pleasure, even to sacrificing their own lives. The greater the refinement of man's awareness, the more clearly he recognizes the quest for enjoyment as a search for inner, divine joy.

Thus, the basic human desire for happiness deserves to be recognized as the cornerstone of the loftiest moral vision.

Backing off from man to consider again the totality of life, we find that the evidence points to a continuity and a harmony, not only in all life, but perhaps in the very universe. Everywhere on this planet, at least, we find a reaching upward: first, toward greater awareness; then, toward greater enjoyment of that awareness; and finally, toward joy itself.

This means, then, that evolution is more than a blind upward push from below, through the ceaseless threats from environment to the survival of a species. Evolution is also a process of *reaching upward* toward fulfillments yet to be achieved. Indeed, evolution deserves to be defined *more* in relation to the heights than to the depths.

Orthodox thinking so far, almost as much so in religion as in science, has viewed mankind—to say nothing of the lower forms of life—almost wholly in relation to the depths. In religion, the emphasis has been on original sin. In physics and chemistry, it has been on the material origins of life. In biology, it has been on the gradual change from lower life forms as a result of the struggle for survival. In psychology, it has been on defining man in terms of his more physical drives, which are merely suppressed when he tries to live by lofty ideals. Always, the emphasis has been on the lower as though it, and not man's aspirations, were the basic reality.

If the force behind life and evolution were nothing but a struggle for procreation and survival, a blind push upwards from below, then certainly we ought to acknowledge this reality humbly, lest we cut ourselves off from the very wellspring of our existence. To deny our primordial urges would mean to weaken any chances we might have for further development.

If, however, the creative force behind evolution has been a search for experience, and for expanding awareness and enjoyment, then it is forward with aspiration, and not backward with fear or deprecation, that man must look for further guidance on the evolutional path.

In fact, the common experience of life at every level, and by no means only the human level, tells us that worthwhile developments are always the result of reaching out for something better, and not of being swept along accidentally like unresisting pebbles in a mountain stream.

Again, the fact that life is capable of evolving to higher levels of awareness means that life's highest potential is the central reality, of which the lower forms are as yet but imperfect manifestations. The lowest life forms may be compared, in other words, to the first, tentative brush strokes on a vast, uncompleted canvas.

Science speaks of potential energy. This is what is

present in a pendulum, for instance, at the top of its swing: Though the pendulum is momentarily motionless, it contains all the energy potential for its downward movement. Life, similarly, contains in its humblest beginnings all the potential for its highest future development—a potential presumably far greater than that realized by mankind up to the present time. Life must, gradually, *of its own nature,* find its way to higher and higher manifestations of awareness.

In the ancient Indian epic, *The Mahabharata,* Krishna, symbolic of the divine consciousness in man, agrees to remain at Arjuna's side during the war of Kurukshetra. He does so, however, with the stipulation that he will serve only as Arjuna's charioteer, and take no active part in the conflict. Arjuna is pleased with the arrangement, for he is convinced that with the Lord by his side, whether or not actively intervening, victory will be assured.

This allegory might well be applied to organic evolution. Certainly there is no overt sign of divine intervention evident in the long, tortuous, and apparently haphazard process of natural selection. And yet, the very presence of life itself has been virtually a guarantee of development, sooner or later. No conscious goal was required, no omniscient guide to blaze the evolutionary trail. Quite sufficient—and far more marvelous, surely—has been the innate urge of life itself to experience, to explore, to understand, to enjoy—and, ever more fully, through self-expression, to discover its own highest potential.

The greatest artist is always the one who allows his

creations in a sense to "create" themselves, to work out their own destinies, without the imposition of his own predetermined ends and inclinations. If the human creator gives his creations so much latitude for self-expression, is it not impious—to echo Simpson's sarcasm back to him—to impute less sensitivity to the Cosmic Creator toward His universal handiwork?

But again, if the highest achievements are already present *as a potential* even at life's humblest beginnings, this means that the heights have not actually to be created, any more than energy has to be created for the downward swing of a pendulum. The heights of awareness must have existed from the beginning. And the forms of life that have evolved have been vehicles, only, for the increasing *manifestation* of consciousness—a consciousness which, in itself, has remained ever present, and ever constant.

In this sense, there has been no actual evolution, no progress, no process of becoming. There has been only a gradually increasing realization of the fullness of that which was from the beginning.

A speculative question, perhaps, in the present context, but certainly a most challenging one.

The vital question remains: What *are* we? What is man?

CHAPTER THIRTEEN

In Search of an Absolute

In the expansion of awareness we've discerned a universal criterion of progress. Given awareness as a yardstick, one cannot help wondering where its limits lie.

At its highest observable levels, we see a shift away from definitions and toward a more unitive vision. Might total awareness, then, entail the disappearance of distinctions and relativities altogether, resulting in a state of consciousness that is absolute?

CHAPTER THIRTEEN

In Search of an Absolute

I regard consciousness as fundamental. I regard matter as derivative from consciousness.

—Max Planck

The great sage Paramhansa Yogananda was once asked, "Is there any end to evolution?"

"No end," he replied. "You go on until you achieve endlessness."

WHAT ARE WE?
WHAT IS MAN?

A common notion since Darwin's time has been that man, being an animal, and having descended from primitive life forms, is only incidentally different from the other creatures with which our planet teems. Man's lower self represents him as he truly is.

Does he love beauty? That's all right, but let him not forget that love of beauty derives from animal desires that are essentially sexual, not spiritual.

Does wisdom inspire him? No harm, so long as he realizes that his desire for wisdom is rooted in an ego-lust for power, derived still more deeply from the instinct of self-preservation.

Sex, power, survival: These are life's bare realities. Lofty ideals are nothing but frills, gracefully draped to conceal the coarse, earthy facts, much as an ungrateful daughter, after marrying advantageously, might refuse to recognize her poor parents.

It follows naturally from such a view that sorrow and frustration must befall him who strives too earnestly to rise above his origins. (A common expression matches this statement: "He's getting above himself.") Mud we are, and mud we must remain. Or, as a chemist or a physicist might put it, chemicals we are, and chemicals we must remain; or, as a biologist might, animal drives and instincts we are, and animal drives and instincts we must remain. The human race is nothing higher. There is no grand truth toward which we may aspire, except perhaps in imagination. The very word, "progress," is rooted in self-delusion. There are only infinite variations on an old, old jungle theme.

Such is the common, or perhaps one should say the educated, view. We have seen, however, that it is untenable. The petty view of mankind is born of too close familiarity. It reminds one of the words of Jesus Christ: "A prophet is not without honor, save in his own country." When one stands too close to a painting, all he can see is the brush strokes; the overall theme is lost to his gaze. It is natural, similarly, when the study of man is directed toward his origins, for his potential for greatness to get overlooked.

But the truth is that man can be better understood in

relation to his potentials than to his beginnings. The first brush strokes on a canvas are more relevant to the end results of the painting than to the blobs of paint on the artist's palette. And the artist works with his mind more on what he hopes to achieve than on the efforts that have brought his painting to its present state of development.

Let us for a moment, just for the sake of argument, accept the opposite argument and search our origins for the "true me." At what point ought we to stop? Sex and ego drives are a part of our animal nature; it is at least arguable that our artistic tendencies and high ideals, such as they may be, derive from them. Proceeding still farther down the ladder of evolution, however, we find sex and ego going the same route as our artistic tendencies and ideals. The sex drive becomes reduced to asexual reproduction; the ego, to a state of awareness so dim and so lacking in definition that it can scarcely be considered self-aware.

Moving still further down the ladder, asexual procreation vanishes also; organic movement ceases; and we are left at last with the immobility and nescience of the rocks.

Shall we say, then, that artistic tendencies and high ideals derive from a frustrated desire to remain immobile and unaware?

Obviously, it would be impossible to trace high aspirations back to their first point of origin. By the same token, who could imagine their point of ultimate development?

One often hears the expression, "It's *absolutely* perfect!" Strictly speaking, of course, it isn't correct to describe anything in a relative universe as perfect, let alone as "absolutely" so. Yet the possibility of absolute perfection certainly lingers on deeper-than-rational levels of human expectation. How eagerly the mind strains outward to embrace infinity! Voltaire put it well when he wrote, "If God did not exist, it would be necessary to invent Him."

We have seen that, for the overall scheme of things to be meaningful to man, it is not essential to posit an Absolute. The only necessity for a continued sense of purpose is for us to continue to expand our awareness from whatever our present limitations may be. The human spirit, however, is far too adventurous to be satisfied for long with taking little steps. It flies ahead, impatient to imagine what it cannot see beyond the horizon.

As human beings, we seem hopelessly ensnared in a web of relativity. It is human nature, however, and perhaps also the very instinct of life, to grope toward a state of fulfillment which we identify, if only subconsciously, with ultimate perfection.

It seems likely that one reason why mankind grows in understanding so much more rapidly than the lower animals is not only because he is more intelligent, but also because he has a tendency to set himself goals in life. By goal-orientation he ceases to be vague, and becomes more focused on progress. Even a horse increases its speed as it approaches the stable.

Probably, then, while the concept of an absolute is not strictly necessary to humanity in its evolutional progress, such a concept can inspire a more forceful upward aspiration.

In the last chapter we identified evolutional progress with progressively expanding awareness. Observing this expansive process at its earliest stages of evolution, we find, as life evolves, a growing consciousness of distinctions among diverse phenomena. At the human stage of evolution, however, the process is reversed: Distinctions begin progressively to disappear.

The simple paramecium, while sensitive to light, is incapable of visually distinguishing one object from another. As eyesight develops with the appearance of higher forms of life, it enables them to distinguish differences of form and color. As evolution continues upward through the animal kingdom, it is generally marked by the refinement of sensory awareness.

With mankind, however, the process abruptly changes direction. Man, generally speaking, does not see, hear, or smell as well as the lower vertebrates. As human awareness evolves, moreover, it does not as a rule perceive as keenly with the senses as we find with more primitive peoples.

The true test of evolutional progress, then, does not seem to be *sensory* awareness, nor an ability to make objective distinctions; rather, it is *the simple quality of awareness itself.* An Australian bushman will see a cloud of dust on the horizon long before his city visitor has any inkling of its existence. Yet the bushman is not considered thereby more essentially aware.

A bigot will see distinctions between people that would not even occur to a more broad-minded person. A con-man will discern larcenous tendencies in others that may be completely unsuspected by honest people. Expansive awareness is due not so much to an ability to make superficial distinctions as to a broadening of identity, of sympathy and understanding. What distinguishes wisdom in people is their perception of underlying connections between different-seeming phenomena. Above all, it is their vision of the essential unity underlying apparent diversity.

The kaleidoscope of natural phenomena, which to the lowest life forms appear as little more than a blur, and which become increasingly distinct to life forms as they evolve, become once again, at the highest levels of awareness, indistinct—not blurred as at first, but indistinct rather in the sense that distinctions at these levels seem superficial, and therefore relatively inconsequential.

This line of development may be seen in the development of science also. Science busied itself, at first, with identifying and classifying phenomena. This process of classification led in time to the discovery that all phenomena are reducible to a few basic elements. Next came the realization that these basic elements are only variations of a still-more-basic atomic structure, epitomized by the simplest of the atoms, the hydrogen atom. Finally, in the Twentieth Century, came the discovery that the atom itself is only a manifestation of energy. Trees and rocks and water and human beings— all phenomena, indeed, differ from one another only in appearance; as energy, they are essentially one.

Obviously, no scientist would cheerfully bite into a pebble, simply because it is essentially the same thing as a peach. Differences in appearance and function are no less actual. They are, however, superficial, and not inherently relevant.

The same tendency towards a unitive vision may be seen in other lines of development as well. It is a mark of human wisdom, for example, to see unity in apparent diversity; to sense a common bond with others, even with the lowest criminal; to discern connecting principles beneath all the seeming contradictions in human nature. And while similar features in nature, whether human, animal, or mineral, are often discovered on careful investigation to be merely coincidental, yet the inexorable trend of wisdom in every field is not only toward the discovery of relationships, but toward the further realization of a unity inherent in relationships.

Everywhere, the evolution of awareness follows the same path: from vagueness to specificity; from specificity to a recognition of broad similarities; and from the recognition of similarities to a discovery of essential oneness. This last stage is superficially similar to the first. In their degree of actual awareness, however, the two are polar opposites.

Awareness differs from its polar opposite in a practical sense also. For with expanding awareness one gains not only clarity, but power. Clarity is passive, but power is dynamic. Clarity discerns the path to progress, but power is necessary for progress actually to be achieved. In vagueness, power is minimal, which is why vague people so seldom succeed at anything. In expanded awareness on the other hand, with its unitive vision, power is maximal.

At every level of reality, awareness is the master key. A rock, for the person who lacks awareness of the latent power in the atom, can supply him with energy only if he makes a great expenditure of effort to lift and maneuver it, perhaps at last to hurl it laboriously from some sort of machine, like the catapult that was used to break down the ramparts of medieval towns. If one's awareness of the power latent in a rock is limited to its size and weight, the power he can derive from it will be relatively little. Awareness of the rock as energy, however, and knowledge of how to release that energy from its atoms, may make it possible with a minuscule portion of the rock to power an entire city.

On a human level also, those who exert the greatest influence over our lives are those with the fullest awareness of their essential oneness with us—people like Jesus Christ, or, on a more mundane level, men like George Washington, Abraham Lincoln, and William Shakespeare.

The more expansive one's view of reality, the more all-pervading his vision of the unity beneath superficial appearances. We have seen, in the material realm, an infinite number of appearances reduced to a single substance: energy. In other realms, too, the trend is evident: in the psychological, the emotional, the moral, the spiritual. It is well known that love and hatred have much in common. Pleasure and pain, too, are opposite sides of the same coin. And fear, while not normally paired with greed, can yet be rooted in greed, as greed also can be rooted in fear. The rationale behind morality is, as we have seen, the desire to avoid pain and achieve lasting happiness. And all psychological traits derive, finally, from consciousness of the ego.

Is there an end to the potential for expansion of awareness? It would seem that, the less limited awareness is by identification with distinctions, the easier its expansion becomes. Awareness gains power *in itself,* in other words, and not only objectively over nature, as it transcends identification with matter. The more matter fades as an essential reality, the more awareness comes into its own.

With the disappearance of relativities, then, what is left? Clearly, whatever ultimate reality remains must by very definition be absolute.

An Absolute, if it exists, must be totally aware. For every *decrease* in the sense of distinctions involves an expansion, an *increase,* of awareness itself. This inverse ratio, pointing on the one hand to the eventual disappearance of relativity, indicates on the other hand *an absolute confirmation of Self-awareness.*

The ultimate "substance" of reality, in this case, can only be pure consciousness.

Thus far can reason take us. Reason alone, however, can only suggest probabilities; it cannot prove them. Even in suggesting them, however, it does more than point up at the mist concealing the mountaintop and exclaim, "If only one could climb to the top!" For reason suggests also that this absolute state of being, if indeed it exists, *must be available as a conscious experience.* The experience, if available, would constitute proof.

Science, after a prolonged study of the facts available, inferred the existence of the atom. This inference did not in itself constitute proof. Such proof came later, when at last the atom was successfully split.

Similar is the case with awareness. Although reason cannot actually prove the existence of an Absolute, it does enable us to make the strong statement: "If an Absolute exists, it must also be knowable."

Science, with its growing confidence in the atom's existence, redoubled its efforts to prove atomic theory by experiment. The facts, similarly, that we've marshaled in these chapters point so temptingly to the existence of an Absolute that they constitute a veritable clarion call to the adventurous in spirit.

Could there have existed; could there exist even today; or might there exist someday in the future, men and women to whom the Absolute was, is, or will prove to be knowable in terms of actual experience? Is it possible for religious beliefs to be transcended in the actual, direct perception of truth? The very suggestion staggers the imagination.

This, indeed, is the special line of inquiry that has been followed in India since ancient times. It is valid, indeed, to call it the special genius of that civilization. India's approach to reality, which comes to the reasonable conclusion that an Absolute must exist, and that it must be available to man by direct, personal experience, has inspired bold spirits down the ages to dare to attempt the spiritual heights.

In this inward call to adventure we find a close parallel to the call of modern science, to which so many young men and women in recent centuries have responded. The adventurous spirit in science has revolutionized man's relationship to the universe around him, and has given him a measure of power over nature of which mankind formerly never dreamed.

In India, the attempt to scale the heights of awareness

has produced in every century sages who have demonstrated in their own lives a power of love over others, as well as over objective nature, which the average person today would consider miraculous.

The Indian Vedantic experience of the Absolute is of a Supreme Consciousness—"One without a second"—of which the entire universe is a manifestation. In this experience there is no Godhead "wholly other," to quote a favorite expression of Christian theologians; no Creator essentially separate from His creation.

"Spirit sleeps in the minerals," the Indian scriptures aver, "dreams in the plants, in the animals begins to awaken, and in man *knows* that he is awake." The universe is a dream in the Absolute consciousness—real, but only in the sense that it is a manifestation of that consciousness.

Why, one might ask, if all things are essentially divine, are they so manifestly imperfect? The answer is quite simple: With the appearance of manifested forms, relativities, too, make their bow on the stage of appearances. *In this relative realm, the Absolute itself cannot function absolutely.* The very fact of *function,* as opposed to *being,* implies the assumption of relativity. Things and deeds are relative and imperfect by very virtue of the fact that they fall short of the state of Absolute Perfection.

The more consciousness becomes identified with material limitations, rather than with the life energy, which dwells in material forms, the farther down the evolutionary scale, and the farther removed consequently from perfection, it must necessarily be. As the upward movement of evolution is increasingly toward a vision of unity, so the downward movement of consciousness is toward the perception of ever-greater disunity.

Once, however, a man realizes himself as he really is (so the Vedanta teachings claim), he ceases to be conscious of things in terms of their separate individuality and of their consequent imperfection. Conscious at last on a soul level, he perceives himself as eternally one with Infinite Perfection.

Is man, then, God? Though many have drawn this conclusion, it is philosophically absurd to equate the limited expression with the Wholeness to which it belongs. Clearly, nothing in relativity can be equated with the Absolute.

Here, however, is a vital consideration: It cannot be separated from the Absolute, either.

Paramhansa Yogananda, a great sage of India, explained the relation of the Absolute to its creation by drawing a parallel to the ocean and its waves. The ocean is *expressed* in the waves, but is not limited to that expression. Nor is it in any way defined by such expression. As the waves change, the ocean remains essentially the same. One may say that the ocean, at its surface, has become the many waves, but not therefore that the waves are the ocean.

We may say, then, that God has manifested all human beings, but not that human beings are therefore God. The fact of an Absolute at the heart of relativity does not mean that perfection can be claimed for lower levels of awareness. The farther down that scale, the more one's vision of things becomes distorted; one's mental horizons, narrowed.

Many Western religionists, confronted with the teachings of the *Vedanta,* complain, "Well, no doubt it is very fine, philosophically speaking, to imagine an Absolute Consciousness, and perhaps even to think of it as some sort of ocean. But what about *God,* our Heavenly Father, a benign, omniscient Being who loves us and Whom we can love in return—a Spirit to Whom we can pray and offer our adoration?"

This may seem a reasonable objection, but in fact it is disproved by experience. The soul's relationship with the Absolute has been found *by experience* to become increasingly a relationship of love. Reason, moreover, following the path we have opened in this chapter, supports this experience. For as relativities are transcended, Ultimate Love must needs be the only relationship left to the soul. God, the eternal Absolute, Whose consciousness dreamed the very universe into existence, could have no difficulty—and so indeed countless enlightened sages have testified—in relating to human beings in whatever way they themselves hold most dear.

Implicit in those theologians' objection is the thought that the more abstract a thing is, the less it must contain of love, or of feeling of any kind. It must be greater, according to this way of thinking, to limit love to one person than to expand it to embrace everyone. Such an assumption contradicts the very principle we have established of expanding awareness. In fact, when feeling is released from identification with that which it is not, it can only grow, not shrink, in depth, power, and purity.

Jean-Paul Sartre said it for the lower elements in human evolution when he wrote, "To be conscious of another means to be conscious of what one is not." And the *Taittiriya Upanishad* of India said it for the highest with this ringing cry: "The Spirit Who is here in a man, and the Spirit Who is there in the sun, it is one Spirit and there is no other!"

The greater a man is, the more capable he is of deep feeling. Every expansion of consciousness, every broader vision of the unity of all life, brings with it an *increase* of awareness, never a loss. Love, when liberated from bondage to form, comes at last into its own.

Jesus Christ was an example of this truth. He was not attached to anything or to anyone, not even to his closest relatives.* Yet he was known as a man of extraordinary love.

The Buddha, though he renounced his earthly family in his search for truth, became thereby a sage whose compassion still sings to us down the centuries.

"Love is not love which alters when it alteration finds,"† wrote the great Bard. The personal love that people express for one another is usually tainted with selfish conditions. Such love cannot but be inconstant. "I love this woman because her beauty pleases me." "I

---

* "Who is my mother? and who are my brethren? And he stretched forth his hand toward his disciples, and said, Behold my mother and my brethren! For whosoever shall do the will of my Father which is in heaven, the same is my brother, and sister, and mother." (Matthew 12:48–50)

† Shakespeare, Sonnet 116.

love that man because he is so kind to me." When beauty vanishes, or when kindness shifts its attentions elsewhere, what becomes of such "love"?

There was once a courtesan who expressed a physical attraction for the Buddha. The Buddha had long since transcended earthly passions, yet he answered her that he loved her, too. To her pleas that he come to her, he replied, "Not now. Some other time."

One day, long afterwards, the Buddha cried suddenly, "My beloved, the courtesan, needs me! I must go to her." He hastened in the direction of the courtesan's home, his disciples rushing after him in the desperate hope of somehow saving their master from a spiritual fall.

And there he found her at death's door, her body ravaged by disease, her loveliness completely destroyed. All her former friends and lovers had abandoned her.

The Buddha, finding her in this pitiable state, took her head tenderly on his lap. It is said that he healed her, and that afterwards she became one of his most devout disciples. But surely, whether or not such a healing actually occurred, the unconditional nature of his love must have taught her a deep lesson regarding the nature of true love.

For what was his feeling towards her? It was not for her body, but for her soul, of which the body was only a fleeting expression. Buddha had entered the heart of Love itself—Love infinite, Love absolute, because freed forever from ego-defined limitations.

Abstraction implies no loss of feeling. The Absolute, if it exists at all, can only exist in a state of perfection. This would necessarily imply a perfection of love also, and not merely some sort of intellectual mist. Impersonal? Yes, but *more* loving, not less so, in consequence.

Un-personal? Indifferent to us as individuals, with our human problems and woes? But why so? The more even human beings become impersonal in their affections, the more truly they find that they can give of themselves freely to everyone.

Mahatma Gandhi, while tossed on a sea of national crises, was able in an instant to give his full and sympathetic attention to a little child who asked it of him. The Mahatma's love was free. It was his inner freedom which enabled him to give love to another so readily.

The greatness of human beings must point, at least, to the inconceivably vaster greatness of God. A loving Father? He who is everything—why can He not be a Father to us, too—or a Mother, a Friend, a Beloved: any form, indeed, that we ourselves find meaningful—if He so chooses, and if we ask it of Him lovingly?

This is the teaching of India: A God not only impersonal, but personal also—personal more perfectly, because impersonal first.

CHAPTER FOURTEEN

The Law of Transcendence

*Everything is sacred, for with the help of the
outer man attains to the inner.*
—Taittiriya Upanishad

IMAGINE THE WINDLESS SURFACE of a dead sphere in space. Let's call it a planet, for its surface is solid. But there is no sun for it to revolve around. There are no stars anywhere: nothing to which this solitary sphere might be related.

Since comparisons are impossible, one couldn't say that our sphere was large or small, or moving one way or another, or even moving at all. In the absence of other heavenly bodies, it would be impossible even to determine the existence of space.

Let us now conjure into existence one other heavenly body: a sun, stationary above the planet's surface. Both spheres are motionless.

In the complete absence of movement, obviously, there can be no passage of time.

Let us now introduce movement. Imagine the sun rising in the east, arching over the planet, and setting in the west. Time, with this movement, is introduced into the picture. So far, however, it would be impossible to say, in terms of our earth time, whether this planetary day had encompassed a second, a year, or a billion years. Time would exist, but it would as yet have no relative meaning.

Next, let us imagine this planet as our own earth, teeming with all the restless activity to which we people of earth are accustomed: the heaving tides, rolling surf, scudding clouds, lightning flashes, and driving rain; the bright flowers and humble grasses nodding in the wind; the buzzing insects; the brief, swift flight of sparrows, and the slow circling of hawks; the hubbub of human enterprise; the heartbeats and breathing of men and animals; the life and death cycles of all living creatures.

Time, now, would have taken on relativity and would be filled with rich meaning. A day would have become an identifiable time span, very different from a year, from a billion years, and from the fleeting minutes and seconds by which we delude ourselves into imagining that life is long.

Finally, into this kaleidoscope of chronological relativity let us introduce one more factor: thought. Thoughts, for us, have the power to slow time down or to speed it up. Relative to the vibrations of thought, a minute might seem like an hour, or a day be condensed into the brevity of a few minutes.

I remember one morning in college sitting down to write a play. So deep was my concentration that I had the impression only minutes had passed, when I found to my amazement that I had to turn on the light, as the sun was setting. Nine and a half hours had flown by! Such is thought's influence on time.

Travelers commonly experience time very differently from the family members and friends they leave at home. A voyage of one month may seem to them, according to their own time sense, to have taken months.

It is movement which produces time. It may even be that movement and time are synonymous. Is it then movement also which produces space? Space without movement is a meaningless concept, certainly. Movement, rather than static positions in space, is what creates the essence of reality as we know it.

Here, then, is an interesting philosophical conundrum: If a clock is stopped, does it tell the correct time twice a day? Or is it never correct? Philosophically speaking, since time is inextricable from movement, one would have to say that the stopped clock never tells the correct time.

It is consciousness which determines how quickly time passes, since only consciousness attaches values to anything. But it is also consciousness *in motion*—the movement of thoughts, in other words—which makes this value judgment, which gauges objective movement in relation to subjective movement.

Suppose, now, that we were fully conscious, but without thoughts. Would all other movement cease, for us, to exist? Perhaps we would observe movement not as something that occurs in space, but as something that had already occurred: a completed cycle.

The potential energy for the completion of a pendulum's swing exists already before the pendulum is set into motion. We've suggested already in Chapter 12 that for anything to have appeared in the long evolutional climb, it must have existed from the very beginning *as a potential.* Perhaps the same thing is true of movement.

Again and again in the utterances of the truly wise—that is to say, the great men and women of spiritual vision—we encounter the statement that time and space are only mental concepts. One thinks here of the answer Jesus Christ gave to the Pharisees: "Before Abraham was, I *am.*"

A mind that held not the flicker of a moving thought would, on beholding movement, be faced with three alternatives: either to move mentally with that motion, and thus cease remaining motionless; or—but not really conceivably—to see it as a sequence of motionless positions; or else, to see it as an entire cycle, a completion, in which no movement had actually taken place at all, since the cycle existed already in its entirety from the moment of its projection.

A comparison might be made here to a large painting, the whole of which exists already, and can be seen in its entirety from the detached perspective of distance, while anyone standing close to it must take it in a section at a time, as his gaze passes over it in a broad sweep.

Perhaps this is the explanation for the phenomenon of prophecy, which defies common sense and yet has been demonstrated again and again to exist. A commonly reported feature of prophecy is the fact that those with the gift for it often err in the matter of timing. Their error is understandable, if their vision springs from levels of consciousness where movement, as such, doesn't exist, because its cycle is already seen as a wholeness.

The relativity of time and space is an accepted concept in modern physics. Countless other findings of science as well support the idea of a universe rooted, not in things as we experience them with our senses, but in abstract consciousness.

In Chapter One I mentioned modern science's assertion that space is finite. To the layman's perfectly normal question, "If space is finite, what lies outside of it?" science answers: "Nothing. You are applying human concepts to a situation that falls outside of human experience."

And yet, it may be that there is a connection here with human experience after all. A few of the bolder modern scientists, and the entire gamut of India's sages, have described the universe as an idea in the infinite consciousness. Comparing that concept to ideation as we know it, we may say that, however much or little "space" an idea encloses, within its own context, at least, *nothing exists outside of it.* For at that very moment when we ask, "What lies outside?" our thought itself expands with the question. Beyond the confines of that question, quite literally nothing exists.

Seen in this light, the finitude of space offers fascinating evidence for the possibility that the universe really *is* an idea in the infinite consciousness, outside of which, in order for anything to exist at all, the idea itself would have to expand into that nothingness.

Another scientific discovery with spiritual overtones is the Second Law of Thermodynamics. According to this law, everything in the universe is moving toward a state of randomness. Conceived of as a process of gradual disintegration, the Second Law of Thermodynamics is often cited in support of the belief that life, too, is moving away from whatever temporary purpose it might appear to have, toward a state of ultimate chaos and meaninglessness.

And yet, progressive randomness can be interpreted just as reasonably to signify the progressive reversion of all things to that state of oneness and equilibrium which marks the end of relativity, and the apotheosis of consciousness.

By an ever-growing number of paths, scientific research has been reaching a point where the logical next step in mankind's search for truth is an exploration of the stuff of which thoughts themselves are made: consciousness.

The universe we live in is very different from the mechanically structured system our ancestors imagined. And the doctrine of meaninglessness holds the persistent sway it does only because humanity has not yet adjusted to new realities. This process of adjustment might be compared to shifting gears in a car. We are in the neutral interval, while human understanding shifts away from its previous stance. In future, and once understanding has shifted to the new gear, mankind will no doubt feel at least as much at home in this fluid universe as our forefathers did in a seemingly fixed one.

This, in fact, is the only thing we've lost: not meaning, but our traditional definitions of meaning; not the justification for faith, but the solid rock of dogmatism on which people's faith formerly rested. We face now the need to habituate ourselves to thinking more in terms of movement, and less in terms of freezing our realities in eternal poses. The transition may be compared to a shift away from still photography to cinematography.

We must learn to think of matter now as the product of movement, and not of movement the product of matter. For matter *is* vibration—a vibration of energy.

We must learn to think of time, too, more as movement, and less as a series of static events. We must learn, in other words, to see progress as a continuous flow, and the stages of progress as power-vortices where the energy is generated for still further advances.

Stasis in Nature is an illusion. Everything moves. Without motion, the universe itself would simply cease to exist.

To find meaning in a universe of relativities, we must seek it in movement, not in fixed dogmas and definitions. Fixed concepts are useful also, but in the way that pitons are useful in mountain climbing. They can serve us as aids to climbing further. Their definitions, however, and the way we use those definitions, must be transcendental. They must direct us beyond themselves. Otherwise, movement itself will gradually cease, and values of any kind, if not already dead, will be comatose.

This is, in fact, the solution to another of Zeno's logical paradoxes—Zeno, that Greek philosopher whose luckless arrow we discussed in Chapter Five. If anyone had posed him that famous childhood puzzler, "Why does a chicken cross the road?" Zeno would have answered, "It doesn't, because it can't."

He explained, you see, that in order to cross a road

one must first get halfway across it, then half the remaining distance, then half the remainder of that, and so on ad infinitessimum. There is no distance so small that it cannot be halved again. Obviously, then, for the chicken to complete its journey would be impossible.

Reason may be a guiding light, as long as it retains flexibility. In dogmatic old age, however, it becomes a crusty patriarch who will tolerate no contradiction, but who considers it his self-imposed duty to negate every fresh idea.

"Our mind," wrote Alexis Carrel in *Man the Unknown,* "has a natural tendency to reject the things that do not fit into the frame of the scientific or philosophical beliefs of our time. After all, scientists are only men. They are saturated with the prejudices of their environment and their epoch. They willingly believe that facts that cannot be explained by current theories do not exist."[*]

At the farthest boundaries of scientific discovery, spiritual truths are beginning to come into their own.

We are accustomed to believe that science reveals things in their bedrock reality. Indeed, every so often a spokesman for modern science will announce that the fundamentals of the universe are now well established, and that scientists are unlikely to encounter any major new surprises. The smugness of their statements is soon mocked, however, as science continues to make discoveries on all fronts that force the reevaluation, and sometimes the abandonment, of one fundamental tenet after another.

[*] Alexis Carrel, *Man the Unknown* (Harper & Brothers, New York, 1935), p. 40.

The case is wholly different in the realm of spiritual investigation. Here, discoveries have remained essentially the same through the ages. This changelessness is due not to the existence of any sort of ceiling on the capabilities of human understanding, but simply to the fact that absolute truth really *is* absolute.

Science today is no longer even looking for truth. Its concern is with finding workable solutions to problems as they arise. The search for truth is being increasingly relegated there, where it has always belonged: the realm of spiritual inquiry.

Most people identify spirituality with religious orthodoxy. They pay little attention to those inspired individuals for whom spirituality means the direct experience of truth, rather than any system of belief. Most people are not aware, therefore, of the degree to which individuals in this class really do agree with one another on the truths they have experienced.

Never, in any age, civilization, or religion, have these God-realized sages found it necessary to reevaluate, alter, or abandon the central teachings of their predecessors. Where they have challenged orthodoxy, it has only been the misinterpretations of intellect-worshiping priests and theologians, as Jesus Christ challenged the Pharisees. But, as Jesus put it also, "Think not that I am come to destroy the law, or the prophets: I am not come to destroy, but to fulfil." (Matthew 5:17)

These sages are not to be encountered within the framework of any one religion alone. Some of them, indeed, never formally belonged to any religion. The essence of their spiritual experiences, in other words, cannot be accounted for by prior conditioning. Some of them had held beliefs that they found to be in conflict with their later experiences, and that they therefore abandoned. Many of these sages were unfamiliar with some of the basic tenets of their own religions. Many, indeed, were illiterate. Others, on the other hand, were highly learned. For these people have belonged to no particular type of humanity, any more than they have belonged to any one religion. What they have all had in common has been a deep love for God, and unflinching dedication to the truth.

The interesting thing is that all of them have spoken the same spiritual language. Irrespective of broad differences in culture and tradition, and rarely with any knowledge of one another's existence, they not only described the same truths, but often expressed themselves in essentially the same terminology.

Christian missionaries in India, indeed, noting numerous similarities between the Bhagavad Gita (the best-known Hindu scripture) and the Holy Bible, were persuaded that the former must have taken its teachings from the New Testament. The truth is, the Bhagavad Gita was extant in its present form centuries before the time of the New Testament.

In describing spiritual truths, then, let it not be imagined that we are discussing a body of thought that is conjectural, merely. The weight of evidence is, indeed, in certain important respects, far more impressive than in the findings of modern science.

"The Spirit of God moved upon the face of the waters." (Genesis 1:2) Out of absolute consciousness came movement; and out of movement came time, space, relativity, and all the multifarious manifestations of cosmic creation.

Motionlessness lies at the universal cycle's beginning, and also at its end. For each of us to achieve time's end personally, however—that is to say, for us to enter into Absolute Consciousness—we cannot freeze movement artificially by simply refusing to act. Nor is it possible for anyone to achieve Absolute Consciousness by simply holding firm to "absolute" dogmas and definitions. As the Bhagavad Gita puts it, "None can attain the action-less state by merely not acting." Nor, in other words, can motionlessness be achieved by merely refusing to move.

For movement is the very essence of reality as we know it. It cannot be rejected or denied; it must be pressed into active service in our quest for transcendence. The relativity of values must be understood as a directional flow. Because the tendency of analytical reason is to focus on the stages of the journey rather than on the journey itself, we must train our minds to view progress as a flow *through* those stages, without allowing ourselves to become entrenched in any of them.

Consider how the ocean wave rolls toward the shore, causing no corresponding displacement of matter. We might look upon progress, too, as a wave. The constant energy we exert to advance in any field is more important than any stage through which we pass in the process.

The goal of life, then, may be summed up in one word: *transcendence*. Every development suggests its next stage. A beetle reaches out with life-force to experience more of the reality it knows. And so, successively, the beetle becomes a bird, an animal, a human being, a sage. The impulse to transcendence is latent in all life, and takes consciousness beyond the door of death itself to forms that can give it ever-clearer expression. Awareness ever seeks self-expansion. Understanding seeks further understanding. Enjoyment invites more enjoyment. Not to continue developing in these respects is to stagnate; it is to deny the fundamental urge of life.

Ethics, then, should be approached transcendentally also. Our understanding of them needs to grow, and not get mired in fixed definitions. We must understand the principle of expansion, and apply it wisely to every level of life.

Humanity has not waited in darkness all these thousands of years for modern "wisdom" to light its stumbling way out of the caves. It requires little humility to assume that a few valid lessons, at least, must have been learned along the way. Indeed, it would take extraordinary crassness to ignore past tradition while splashing about in a puddle of petty self-conceit, fancying that modern technology alone has all the answers.

Most societies have arrived at basically identical conclusions in their systems of ethics. This fact is enough by itself to suggest that they recognized certain fundamental truths in human nature, rooted, as we've seen, in universal realities. Any society that flies in the face of man's natural desire for inner growth and harmony pays the price that nature exacts of those who flout its laws. That price is physical disease, if the laws broken concern the body. It is mental unbalance and suffering, if the laws broken concern one's relationship to others, and to life. One who barricades himself against the world by pride and selfishness experiences only a state of alienation.

In Chapter One we considered the gypsies of Tuscany, Italy, to whom it is a virtue to lie cleverly. We also considered certain tribes in Africa, among whom kindness is a mark of weakness. We then asked the question that many educated people ask nowadays: Have we the right to call their mores wrong, simply because those differ from our own? The Tuscan gypsies, it must be noted, display no glowing happiness as they lie, or run off triumphantly with other people's wallets. And the African tribes display no enviable trait—no strength of character, for instance—in their disdain for kindness. Actual experience of such people shows them ignorant of certain of nature's basic laws as they apply to human beings.

By untruthfulness one cuts himself off from the broad support he might receive from the very universe. The Tuscan gypsies, for all their cleverness, remain poor, socially outcast, and ineffectual as a people. And those callous African tribespeople, by scorning kindness, inevitably develop a suspicious outlook on the world. For all their vaunted strength, they live in fear of others. Surely that is why black magic plays so important a role in their lives. Nothing in these examples suggests attainment of the fulfillment *those people themselves seek from life.*

The laws of nature govern human conduct as well, and not only more mechanical things such as planetary movements, ocean tides, and changing seasons. Those laws cannot be voted into or out of existence by plebiscite. And because human beings have intelligence, they are capable, if they so choose, of denying the instincts implanted in them by nature. They can also suffer as long as they choose in the prison created by their ignorance.

If the example of entire societies fails to convince, we may study individuals as well: those who, whether knowingly or not, have flouted the laws of nature; and those also who have respected natural law. In all cases, it soon becomes evident that there are principles which, when obeyed, bring harmony both to oneself and to one's relations with the world—but which, when ignored, produce inner turmoil and outer disharmony regardless of anybody's opinions or beliefs.

Among the principles that are rooted in natural law are honesty, truthfulness, kindness, self-discipline, harmlessness, contentment, and non-covetousness. Individuals, as much as nations, that have manifested these principles have found self-integration and happiness, and have been capable of the highest achievements. Those, on the other hand, who denied even one of these qualities have fallen short, at least in that respect, of the greatness they might have known.

These principles are enumerated in every great scripture. There is no need for us, in the experiential approach to truth we have recommended, to turn aside from old trails and blaze new ones. For any path that is followed sincerely cannot but lead in the same general direction. The test of the direction is whether it conduces to increasing transcendence. Reason alone, without the test of experience, is extraordinarily adept at leading people astray. It has done so many times in history, when people were too proud, intellectually, ignoring the counsel whispered to them by their own hearts. Reason need not be abandoned, however, or put gleefully to the sword. Rather, we must use it wisely. Wise use of it begins by uniting reason to the confirmation of calm feeling. Logic must work in conjunction with intuition, and must not presume to walk alone.

In a bar magnet, the molecules, each with its north-south polarity, are so oriented that their poles point north and south instead of haphazardly every which way. If a bar magnet is cut in half, the two parts will possess their own south and north poles, reflecting the magnetic flow within the bar. This molecular alignment couldn't be produced by turning the molecules carefully north and south one by one. Even were this possible, the adjusted molecules would lose their alignment almost as soon as the work of turning them had moved on to other molecules. It is the flow itself that aligns them.

Analytical logic may be compared to carefully turning the "molecules" of thought in the direction one desires. Intuition, on the other hand, is an energy-flow which, passing through those "molecules," magnetizes them. Analytical logic is fragmented and cumbersome; intuition is free-flowing and effortless. If consciousness can be offered freely into the flow of intuition, rather than piecing separate ideas together carefully to form a logical order, it is possible to advance very quickly toward any accomplishment one has in mind.

Moral values, then, as they've been defined in every

scripture and by most societies and governments, are only guidelines. To determine whether they are firmly rooted in natural law—that is to say, whether they match the way things actually work—they must be put to the test of experience. This test concerns the extent to which they promote harmony, happiness, and well-being within man and in his relation to others and to life itself. If they meet this test, they should be taken as *incentives to improvement*, and not stuffed like dead animals, then displayed in glass cases in people's living rooms. If we honor a value without trying to understand it, its value to us will be minimal.

The same is true for values of every kind. For this question includes more than ethics. We value also good health, useful or beautiful possessions, success, inspiration, friendship: The list is endless. In every one of these values, the same principle of directional relativity applies. The good should motivate one to achieve the better, and the better should inspire one toward the best.

An athlete needs to incorporate a variety of positions, carefully thought out, into an overall flow. He must also move mentally, and not only physically, with this flow. To continue focusing on the individual positions after one has learned them would interfere with that flow. The sportsman needs to think in terms of *movement* rather than in terms of a series of static poses.

Nijinsky, the famous Russian ballet dancer, astounded a Swiss ski instructor by duplicating perfectly all his expert twists and turns on a steep mountain slope—movements which the instructor had executed with a view to impressing his guest. Nijinsky had never seen a pair of skis before. His mastery as a dancer, however, of the basic principles of body movement enabled him easily to transcend the predicament of the average novice: how to position elbows and legs, how to shift weight from one ski to the other, how to hold the back and shoulders—preoccupations that cause most neophytes to take many a tumble.

I have been emphasizing the image of forward movement for the sake of illustration, because the mind finds it easier to think linearly. In fact, of course, as I've made clear in earlier chapters, the development of consciousness is not linear, but expansive.

In order to enter into the spirit of continuous expansion, mere intellectual willingness is not enough. The ego must also shed its attachments and desires. Indeed, it would be impossible, no matter how skillful one's logic, for reason to accomplish that expansion without the aid of intuition. For the secret of expansion lies in the heart. If the heart is disturbed by emotions, or if its feelings are arid and lacking in refinement, expansion is not possible. As well might one inflate a toy balloon, held in the hand, without breathing into it. Once the heart's feelings are awakened and focused, however, it is feeling itself that provides the fuel for expansion. The essence of transcendence lies in freeing the heart of emotional impediments and ego-contractive attachments, and in reversing its flow of feeling toward soul-expansion in soaring flights of devotion.

The emotions are our "demons," for they obstruct our growth in understanding. These demons range themselves in grim determination to combat expansiveness and soul-aspiration of any kind.

Earlier, I defined two laws of human nature: "The Law of Dogmatic Proliferation," which I presented half-humorously; and "The Law of Motivation," which is basic in all human striving. Our discourse would not be complete without the addition of a third law: "The Law of Transcendence."

The first one, **The Law of Dogmatic Proliferation,** was stated thus (as the reader may recall): *The dogmatic tendency increases in direct proportion to one's inability to prove a point.* Behind all exaggerated assertiveness there hovers a cloud of uncertainty and doubt. This first law challenges us to base our understanding on actual experience, not on untested theories.

The second one, **The Law of Motivation,** is universal to all conscious existence. It was stated thus: *Beneath every sensory desire is the deeper urge to avoid pain, and to experience pleasure; and beneath every deeper, heart's desire is the longing to escape sorrow, and to attain permanent happiness.*

The third one, **The Law of Transcendence,** follows naturally after these others. It takes human consciousness beyond fixed ideas, and beyond people's basic motivation for action, to an inevitable conclusion: the state—permanent, not fixed and rigid—of harmony with truth, and fulfillment, at every level, of the Law of Motivation. This third law may be stated as follows: *The ultimate goal of action is freedom from the very need to act.*

We all seek permanent happiness. No one has, as his long-term goal, a happiness that is evanescent. Permanent happiness can be attained only in absolute consciousness. This state of perfect bliss lies beyond striving. As St. Augustine put it, "Lord, Thou hast made us for Thyself, and our hearts are restless until they find rest in Thee." Rest, in a spiritual sense, altogether transcends the temporary repose granted by subconsciousness. It is, for one thing, an infinite *increase*, not a diminution, of awareness. For another, it is calm and forever undisturbed by dreams of further fulfillment. And for a third, it is superconscious: complete and blissful in itself.

Ego-motivated action seeks rest of a different kind, though it counts as rest all the same. For it hopes in fulfillment to achieve the end of that particular form of striving. One pursues a desire with the purpose of finding release from that desire. Activity is a means to that restful end.

Activity may also, of course, seem an end in itself. Skiing is a good example: a form of activity sought and enjoyed for its own sake. Even so, what one subconsciously wants is something more than strenuous movement: a kind of weightless freedom, perhaps, and a transcendence of body-consciousness. Pursued further, this bodilessness would eventually lift one to omnipresence and absolute rest. In any case, the desire for rest is implicit in every movement, and cannot be dismissed by transitory excitement as so many people try to do.

Both kinds of action, therefore, whether spiritual or desire-motivated, have essentially the same goal: transcendence in a state of rest. Desire-motivated activity, however, achieves its end only fleetingly, soon turning back again to restlessness of heart and mind. That seaside cottage one has dreamed of, with breeze-blowing roses and the freshness of sea air, becomes boring after a time. Outward fulfillment, if sought to excess, constricts the ego and suffocates its deeper aspirations.

Spiritually motivated action, on the other hand, is expansive of its own nature. It frees a person's consciousness from its bondage to ego, and brings ever-increasing inner peace. To the extent, moreover, that spiritual action lacks ego-motivation, it leads toward union with infinite consciousness. The Law of Transcendence, then, is the key to freedom: conscious, blissful freedom in an end to all striving.

Freedom increases to the degree that one is motivated by a desire for expanding awareness, which includes expanding sympathy.

It is in contact with the deeper Self, or soul, that the natural urge to self-expansion comes into its own. Ego-consciousness belongs in the realm of relativity, but true transcendence is achieved in that deep state of consciousness which is the very heart of existence, and is beyond relativity.

Everything points to the conclusion that man is innately divine. Psychologists rightly claim that full self-integration cannot be achieved by suppressing one's true nature. The Bhagavad Gita makes this statement also, stating: "All beings, even the wise, follow the ways dictated by their own natures. What can suppression avail?" (III:33) The kind of suppression of which people are particularly guilty, however, is not that which concerned Freud. Sigmund Freud declared that people suppress their true nature when they pretend to possess noble or uplifting qualities. Humanity, he claimed (following the discoveries of Charles Darwin), is the outcome of an upward thrust from below, not of a divine call from above. If we would live "honestly," Freud insisted, we should abide by our animal impulses. If anything, what we should suppress are our higher aspirations, for anything loftier than our present state is merely fanciful, if not dangerous, for the delusions it encourages, to our mental health.

In this thought, those psychologists who accept his influence have erred greatly. Their teaching encourages bondage to emotion and ego. The way of escape lies not, in any case, in redefining one's personality, but in transcending it. Lasting relief will not be found by wandering from one room of ego-consciousness to another, but only by returning to the divine simplicity that is everyone's true nature. For this achievement, one must leave that house altogether.

The entire universe is full of meaning—a meaning that can never be defined, for mere words are utterly unequal to the task. It is the heart that recognizes meaning. The intellect, when not balanced by feeling, is incapable of such insight. Meaning can be experienced, but it can never be reduced to a formula. It is relative, yes, but it is by no means chaotic. Nor, therefore, is truth a matter of mere opinion. Indeed, the very relativity of meaning is directional. Our understanding of it develops experientially, like a mountain goat leaping upward from crag to crag. This directionality, while not absolute, is *universal*. It becomes absolute when individual consciousness merges in Absolute Consciousness.

Meaninglessness, therefore, which modern intellectuals have paraded as a new "truth," is seen to be no challenge to true values at all, but the merest of vagrant superstitions.

To someone, then, who is sincerely seeking truth, the question comes at last: How could matters possibly be otherwise? The very analysis of which those intellectuals are so proud has no essential meaning. Since it is purely intellectual, it is wholly without love or joy. Lacking these, can they really expect to find meaning in anything?

Our discussion of meaning, then, need not be limited to that indefinable abstraction, consciousness. There exists another, irreducible demand placed upon us by nature herself. We have named it already. It is the fact that our impulse toward expanded awareness is invariably accompanied by another: a desire for greater *fulfillment*, and therefore for ever-greater love and joy.

For fulfillment must finally be recognized in terms of *enjoyment*. If it is defined merely as material success, it soon becomes worthless to us. More than anything else, what we want of life is escape from pain, and the attainment of joy. The deeper our joy, the more deeply meaningful our lives become also. The duty with which we are charged by life itself is to find that "hidden treasure": infinite joy and bliss.

Joy boundless! Bliss eternal! Were we to speak in these terms to the average "man in the street," he would dismiss us as absurdly "visionary." ("What are you trying to sell?" he might ask.) Yet we have seen that true realism demands a view of life from the heights of expansive sympathy, not from the depths of cynicism and self-involvement. Clarity and perspective come far more clearly with breadth of vision than with ego-contractiveness. Bitterness and cynicism are not, as many believe, the hallmarks of realism. They reveal only an unwillingness to face reality. They are indications of a selfish heart, and of a mind absorbed in petty self-conceit. Realism demands openness to the universe—that is to say, to what *is*—in forgetfulness of the little self and its petty demands.

The true signs of realism are not contempt, but respect; not bitterness, but appreciation; not ruthless ambition, but kindness and compassion.

This, then, is the meaning of life: not some sterile new doctrine, but continuous development of the heart's feelings toward joyous, ever-conscious experience: perpetual self-transcendence, unending self-expansion—until, in the words of Paramhansa Yogananda, "you achieve endlessness."

ABOUT THE AUTHOR

J. Donald Walters is widely considered one of the foremost living experts on Eastern philosophy and spiritual practice. An American born in Rumania and educated in England, Switzerland, and America, Walters studied at Haverford College and Brown University. He speaks nine languages and has lectured in five of them.

Walters', books and music have sold over 2.5 million copies worldwide and are translated into 24 languages. He has written more than 70 books and composed over 400 pieces of music.

INDEX

THE PROMISE OF IMMORTALITY
IN THE BIBLE AND THE BHAGAVAD GITA
J. Donald Walters

Destined to become a classic, *The Promise of Immortality* is the most complete commentary available on the parallel passages in the Bible and India's ancient scripture, the Bhagavad Gita. This groundbreaking book illuminates the similarities between the scriptures of the world's two most populous religions, vibrantly bringing each to life.

Walters sheds light on many of the famous passages from both texts, showing their practical relevance for the modern day and their potential to help us achieve lasting spiritual transformation.

His elucidation of the ancient texts inspires us with convincing answers to questions long considered imponderable, such as:

• Why is everyone destined to become "Christ-like"?
• Why are "good works" alone not enough?
• Why is love the most powerful force?
• What is the true meaning of the "Golden Rule"?
• Are material desires spiritually harmful?
• What is the best way to read the scriptures?
• How do I find a true teacher?

The Promise of Immortality clarifies apparent differences in religious teachings to reveal a timeless, underlying truth. Walters makes a convincing case for the potential unity of all religious belief, and the possibility of an unprecedented era of cooperation among the world's religions.

THE ART OF SUPPORTIVE LEADERSHIP

A PRACTICAL GUIDE FOR PEOPLE IN POSITIONS OF RESPONSIBILITY
J. Donald Walters

A Proven Approach to Successful Leadership

Do you want to improve your leadership skills and learn how to bring out the best in your employees, co-workers, or students? Then The Art of Supportive Leadership can help you! Large and small companies of every kind—from well-established industrial corporations to sparkling new tech firms— are using this proven approach to leadership with great success. It has become equally indispensable to the nonprofit organizations, schools, and military personnel who also use it.

The Art of Supportive Leadership is defining the new cutting edge of leadership training. Drawn from the author's many years of successful leadership in numerous contexts, the book gives you clear and practical techniques that quickly produce results—even if you're new to leadership, and even if you can only devote limited time to improving your skills. Each chapter ends with short, concise summaries that serve as quick reference guides when you need them.

Learn How to:
- Develop an inspiring vision
- Avoid ego games
- Win the loyalty of others
- Achieve lasting results
- Combine intuition with common sense
- Run ahead of the pack
- Build an effective team
- Find creative solutions to difficult problems

The Art of Supportive Leadership *stands out among business books. I recommend it—it makes for good reading and a good message.*
—Executive Book Summaries

The Art of Supportive Leadership *is brief, hits the points, and has a lot of common sense to it. We've been casting about for something like this for a long time. We use it in our Managers Training Workshop. This book is very practical, very readable, and concise. HIGHLY RECOMMENDED.*
—Kellogg Corporation

ART AS A HIDDEN MESSAGE

A GUIDE TO SELF-REALIZATION
J. Donald Walters

Art as a Hidden Message offers a blueprint for the future of art, and shows how art can be a powerful influence for meaningful existence and positive attitudes in society. With insightful commentary on the great musicians, artists, and creative thinkers of our time, *Art as a Hidden Message* presents a new approach to the arts, one that views both artistic expression and artistic appreciation as creative communication. J. Donald Walters shows the importance of seeing oneself and all things as aspects of a greater reality, of seeking to enter into conscious attunement with that reality, and of seeing all things as channels for the expression of that reality.

Art as a Hidden Message *is a monumental work, and should be required reading for everyone. Artists, especially, will benefit from it, and should carefully read, study, and act on what is enshrined in these pages. This book is, I believe, the most important book of our time on this vitally important subject.*

> **—Derek Bell,** legendary harpist of the five-time Grammy award–winning group The Chieftains

J. Donald Walters has provided a manual for creativity as spiritual practice. Insightful, inspiring and imaginative, **Art as a Hidden Message** *reveals the sacred dimension of artistic expression and opens a new world of meaning and purpose.*

> **—Michael Toms,** co-founder of New Dimensions Radio; co-author of *True Work: The Sacred Dimension of Earning a Living*

HOPE FOR A BETTER WORLD!

THE COOPERATIVE COMMUNITIES WAY
J. Donald Walters

Hope for a Better World! is an impassioned, cogent argument for how each of us, at our very core, is designed to thrive in cooperative environments. Walters both critiques and expands upon the viewpoints of many of the greatest thinkers of Western culture including Plato, Copernicus, Malthus, Machiavelli, Adam Smith, Darwin, Marx, and Freud. He concludes this intellectual tour-de-force with a clarion call for how each of us can best live up to the potential within us and how a new emphasis on building cooperative community environments can help us to achieve this goal.

For a free Crystal Clarity catalog, or to place an order,
please call 800-424-1055 or 530-478-7600.
Or visit our website: www.crystalclarity.com